THE MEANING OF GOD

THE MEANING OF GOD

And Other Selected Pastoral Letters of Emmanuel Cardinal Suhard

Foreword by
SALLY WHELAN CASSIDY

Introduction by
JOHN J. WRIGHT, D.D.

Fides Publishers, Inc.
NOTRE DAME, INDIANA

This DOME edition of *The Meaning of God* and other selected pastoral letters of Emmanuel Cardinal Suhard is reprinted from *The Church Today*, copyright 1953, Fides Publishers Association. The pastoral letters of Cardinal Suhard were originally published in France by *Imprimerie Lahure*, Paris.

The translation of *The Meaning of God* was obtained through the courtesy of the Rev. John Fitzsimmons, London, England.

Assistance in the preparation of the translation of the other pastoral letters was generously given by Dr. Charles Parnell and Mr. Frank Gwyn of the University of Notre Dame.

Printing History
Original Edition 1949
2nd Edition 1953
DOME BOOK EDITION 1963
2nd Printing 1964

All Rights Reserved
Fides Publishers, Inc.
Notre Dame, Indiana

Manufactured by North State Press, Inc., Hammond, Indiana

CONTENTS

page	
7	Foreword
13	Introduction
19	The Meaning of God
65	God's Providence
79	The Parish Community
93	The Christian Family

Foreword

When Cardinal Suhard died the Catholic community felt a shock. The Archbishop of Paris was known in America largely because of his two great pastoral letters, *Growth or Decline?* and *The Meaning of God*. To some he was known as the protector of a revolutionary movement of worker-priests. A few of us had the opportunity of meeting him, of hearing his quiet voice, of quickening to his dynamism, of living in his Paris.

Born in 1874, in stanchly Catholic Brittany, Emmanuel Suhard had the usual career of a French bishop. Noted for his intelligence in the preseminary, he was sent to Rome for his major work, coming back to the major seminary as professor once the S.T.D. had been conferred. Almost none of the French hierarchy have had pastoral experience; the steps in the ladder are nearly always "professor"—"secretary to the Bishop"—"Bishop."

Emmanuel Suhard was named Bishop of Bayeux-Lisieux in 1928. Though he remained there only two years, Lisieux was marked as the future center of the *Mission de France*. The Bishop already had made his reputation as a discerning student of men, as a pastor acutely aware of the personal vocation of each of his priests.

He established a special position, "Adviser on Ecclesiastical Affairs," and charged this adviser with the spiritual formation of the younger priests. They could come to him with full confidence and he would plead their cause before the diocesan authority. Suhard said, "For a long time a bishop in curia has had a chancellor charged with dispensing justice. It is good that he should have another priest charged with dispensing mercy."

After a term of ten years as Archbishop of Reims, in 1935 the cardinalate was bestowed on the man who in 1940 was to step into the great Cardinal Verdier's shoes. Difficult enough to be the Archbishop of Paris, greatest though not the oldest of Gaul's dioceses; to be the successor of Verdier (the man who gave Paris a hundred new churches, who gave thousands of workers jobs during the height of the depression), but worse

* The foreword appeared in October, 1949, issue of "The Catholic World." FIDES acknowledges the kind permission to reprint it here.

still, Emmanuel Cardinal Suhard became Cardinal of Paris during the height of the debacle, the year of France's shame.

During the occupation Suhard made no spectacular name for himself. Only old, ailing Archbishop Saliège of Toulouse kept the name of the French hierarchy from taint of collaboration. Many were those who were dissatisfied with Suhard's role, which was simply to enable the Church to endure, to survive the onslaught. His quiet, precise letter about Conscript Labor was not vigorous enough for them: no ringing phrases, no audacious challenge. Cardinal Suhard was looked upon at best as non-political, a man of prudence, unwilling to take a stand in France's greatest crisis.

With the liberation, a cardinal's hat was sent to Saliège, and a few outstanding Vichyite bishops withdrew into monasteries. Emmanuel Suhard stayed in his place, enduring the scorn, often the open disrespect of younger resistance heroes—uncomplaining, humble, suffering.

Only now that he is dead do we know that he protected the underground Catholic Action movements, the clandestine newspaper *Témoignage Chrétien*; that he risked his life interceding for Jews, hostages, and deportees; that he repeatedly refused to denounce Communism publicly without at the same time denouncing its twin, totalitarianism.

Almost imperceptibly, the Church of France began to stir. Paris was the center of this activity. The wise said, "The Cardinal is allowing this activity because it would go on despite him; he is trying to redeem himself by letting the young act. They, the pride of the resistance, will bring back honor to the Church in France."

Now we know that in the midst of the occupation, Suhard had read a report of two of his priests on the de-Christianization of France. (This report was subsequently published as *France, Pays de Mission;* in English, *France Pagan?*) Now we know that this sexagenarian spent three sleepless nights wrestling with the awful weight of this new realization and rose up transformed. The prudent, gentle man became a Paul calling for audacity, for confidence.

The great Prince of the Church continued his functions.

Mass in celebration of the liberation of Paris, the reception of General LeClerc and his staff, the trumpets of the great army which redeemed France blaring forth at Notre Dame were unforgettable experiences.

But the old Cardinal began to appear in quite other surroundings: young couple's homes, workers' kitchens. Priests and militants of the proletarian missions had ready access to him. They were told: "My life as Archbishop cloisters me here and cuts me off from humanity in its sufferings, hopes, sins and virtues. You must help me, inform me, make me know my people and meet them. How can I be the guardian of the city, the Good Pastor, if you don't help me to know my sheep? Do you realize that you are responsible with me for my bishopric, my diocese?"

The story goes that his secretary would call up and say, "Come when you can: early in the morning, after supper, Saturday afternoon. The Cardinal of Paris will adjust his schedule to your free time." Abbé DePierre himself tells of arriving late for an appointment, and being told, before he had time to excuse himself, "Your role is to serve the workers and to be completely ready to help them. My role is to serve you and to be ready to help you."

Was this simply an imprudent about-face, a flaunting of all traditional roles, the vagary of an old man? What was this living paradox of prudent youth and audacious old age? Cardinal Suhard showed an amazing confidence in his priests and militants, saying, "Go ahead, go ahead, don't stop. The life of the Church is at stake. She asks you to take this step into a world so much in need of unity and collective kindness."

Wise and prudent pastor, he demanded of them charity, piety, devotion, and total giving of self, prudence, doctrine, discipline. He gave them a superior, the wise priest, Abbé Hollande. Only two rules bound them: absolute obedience to the hierarchy and to the laws of team life.

The Cardinal would say: "Together you have the grace of your state of life to enable you to decide about the demands of your apostolate. As long as they do not touch the laws of the liturgical, spiritual, canonical, or doctrinal life of the Church

... you know that there are permissions that you must not ask of me. Have you not received the Holy Spirit? What is the use of your baptism and confirmation, your interior life, and your team life?"

Cardinal Suhard exhorted his priests to live in such a fashion that their lives "could be understandable only if God exists ... witnesses not by superficial change of habits, but by a firm desire to share the destiny of the disinherited masses. A life which was neither an evasion, nor a study of customs, nor even a conquest ... it is a vocation of redemption. Work for them is not a pretext, or propaganda, it is the naturalization act of the priest in a people where he is only a stranger, it is the suffering and penitent sharing of the worker's condition in life."

He was always careful to make clear his confidence. For example, in his warning to the Christian Progressives against "habitual and profound collaboration with the Communists," he ended by saying, "we count more than ever on our priests and militant laymen. Living with the workers, they share their anxieties, their worries, and also their hopes. They have our confidence; all the faithful should know this, and we are happy to reaffirm it."

Few things made Cardinal Suhard more angry than pot shots at the *Mission de Paris*, the apple of his eye. He was an unusually tolerant man who bore with many outdated diocesan institutions and revivalist Catholic movements that he disliked, saying, "there is place for them in the Church, if they allow others to exist. I don't think that I should be more severe than the Pope." An undiscriminating attack on the *Mission*, the integrity of the militants or its action, occasioned some of the few holy rages the Cardinal vented during those years.

Suhard's sense of urgency for the proletarians was only equaled by his concern for the intellectuals. He thought both groups vital in the rebuilding of Catholic France.

The Cardinal awakened the Catholic intellectual institutions (associations, universities, and research institutes) out of their Rip Van Winkle sleep. Under his benevolent interest and protection, Catholic intellectuals began to bestir themselves about the university apostolate. Groups of eminent men with varied

FOREWORD

training met together about a common problem, and the *Centre Intellectuel des Catholiques Français* became a veritable hive of activity, conferences and incisive debates recalling the flash and thrust of the medieval defense of theses.

The intellectual militants were freed by Suhard from the perpetual look-over-the-shoulder, am-I-orthodox fear. His pastoral letter, *Growth or Decline?*, could be called the Catholic intellectual's Magna Charta. In it the Cardinal affirms that intellectual work "remains independent. [The Church] has no mission to solve directly technical problems. She recognizes the legitimate autonomy of competent authorities."

He allayed the intellectual's twofold fear, "Must I give up my professional integrity in research," and, "Is my research really worth while?" by maintaining, "Your research must bear first on pure truth and disinterested science . . . you must not involve any consideration of interest be it even apologetical in your work: you must seek only what is. Your integrity must only be equaled by your open-mindedness and your effective co-operation with all those believers and unbelievers who pursue the truth with all their soul. Do not hesitate to give yourself entirely to the joy of knowing, to your vocation of scholars."

Cardinal Suhard's last public address was made at the annual meeting of Catholic intellectuals where he said, "We live in a great epoch where Catholic intellectuals play a more and more important role. . . . We do not find ready-made answers in the Gospels, in the domain of science, philosophy, social doctrine, art and civilization." He warned them against "premature, *a priori* synthesis," and said that perhaps the next synthesis to illumine future ages as did Augustine's and Thomas's would be a work of another order, the collective work of a group of intellectuals, the end product of many different projects.

Yet the apostolate, the rebuilding of the city, must be the work of all men of good will, not only that of proletarians and scholars. It is the living of Christ among men, the bearing witness, not the retreat into fortresses, or a propaganda campaign.

Cardinal Suhard traces the essential lines of this universal Catholic vocation. It must be "based on Catholic Action," that is to say, be fundamentally the responsibility of the laity. It must be "based primarily on the working class" for two reasons: this is the class most cut off from Christ and the class which is just arriving at adulthood, beginning to take its rightful place in the City. It must be based in the community, because "militants cannot without danger or futility stay alone," and second, because the apostolate must be that of the team, its aim to penetrate groups, institutions, with the life of Christ.

Finally Suhard gives the marks of a true apostolate. It must be realistic, competent, sensible. It must be filled with a "supernatural sense of souls . . . a spirit of faith and humility." It must have persevering charity and, most important of all, "a profound love of the Church."

—Sally Whelan Cassidy

Introduction

One of the most pathetic stories to come out of the French chapter of the history of World War II was a story which a Colonel of the French Army told me personally. It concerns a young man, a partisan of the resistance movement, who was killed by a bullet which ricocheted in the Rue du Bac.

The fatal bullet felled the maquis, described as being in his late teens, in the gutter not far from the convent where St. Catherine Labouré saw with her eyes of flesh the Blessed Mother of God. Within a square mile of the spot there are world-famed churches, shrines and other hallowed places which pilgrims journey from afar to visit. Within sight of each end of the street are monumental evidences of the Christian faith that has been preached in Paris these seventeen centuries and more.

And yet, when two Catholic sisters drew the dying body of this boy into a doorway which might shelter his last moments, they were sickened at heart by the answer the young lad gave to an earnest effort to prepare him for an eternity that was then but seconds away so far as he was concerned.

"Do you love God with all your heart?" one of the religious asked the gasping partisan. *Aimez-vous le Bon Dieu?*

The answer came in accents of pain, embarrassment and confusion. *Comment dirai-je que je L'aime? Je ne Le connais pas de tout, ce Bon Dieu dont tu parles!*

"How shall I say that I love Him? I don't even know who He is, this God of Whom you talk!"

Where was he dying, the mortally wounded young soldier? Not in Borneo, nor in the Arctic, nor at the furthermost ends of the earth beyond the reach of priests or the influence of the Gospel. Not in "mission" country in the usual sense of that too restrictive term. Not in one of the lands which the Propagation of the Faith magazines describe as "pagan" and for which they ask our apostolic alms and prayers.

Not at all. He was dying in the Archdiocese of Paris, *la ville lumière*, capital city of Christian France, rival of Rome itself among the centers of Western Christendom as the centuries since the thirteenth, certainly, have understood Christendom.

He was dying within the shadow of a chapel to which the devout flock by the thousands. He was prostrate in a street along which saints have walked, a street in which many of us have seen great preachers come and go and pilgrims gather for prayer.

Whence did he come, this lad who could not bring himself to declare his love for God because he did not know enough about Him to call upon Him in the hour of death? Was he from the French colonial empire? Had he been born and brought up in the remote wildernesses of the Senegalese? Again, not at all. He was from Paris, where the very stations of the underground railroad, the *Metro*, more often than not bear the names of Catholic saints, so that the stops called out in his ears as he went to and from his school or work were a veritable litany of the saints and catalogue of the Christian dogmas. His home was Paris, a city in which it would be impossible to walk a half mile and not see in one direction or another the towers of a cathedral, the domes of a basilica or the spires of a great church. In all probability, he himself bore the names of two or more saints; it is even likely, too likely, that if he swore in his moments of youthful anger or violence, he invoked the titles of Catholic devotion and blasphemed with the phrases of Catholic faith.

But when he lay dying, with two Catholic sisters striving to comfort his body and elicit the act of charity by which he might save his soul, he cried out in empty, perhaps even bitter agnosticism, his ignorance concerning God. "How shall I say that I love Him? I don't even know who He is, this God of Whom you talk!"

Is he not exceptional, this tragic young man of the Rue du Bac? We who love France, and who love souls even more, wish that we might think so. Alas, he is all too typical of those unnumbered throngs of people, young and old, who comprise the so-called "de-Christianized" populations of France. Paris has them in multitudes; almost every corner of France has some, certain parts of the country have them in frightening numbers.

INTRODUCTION 15

Each of the great cities is heavy of heart, sometimes almost perceptibly so, with its host of unbelievers, the *non-croyants* among the sons and daughters of this land so beloved of the Mother of God and so fruitful in martyrs, missionaries, saints and devout souls of every class and condition.

The dying young man who did not even know who God is and who could not muster enough of grace to call out to Him in love seems to some critics of contemporary France to be the type of a nation which has suffered so many ravages in her body at the hands of militarists and in her soul at the hands of philosophers (of a sort) and politicians. These critics can make out an impressive case for their thesis that France has become "pagan," that the eldest daughter of the Church has proved wayward and derelict. But their case is specious, for all its evidence, and their requiems over the dead soul of Catholic France fortunately are premature.

The France of King St. Louis still lives. So does that of Saint Joan, St. John Vianney, St. Margaret Mary, St. Therese of Lisieux and all the company of the Catholic French saints. France has become the testing place of certain of the most inhuman and disastrous ideas of modern times, from those of the atheists among the political revolutionaries to those of the degenerates among pseudo-intellectuals. All this is true, and its toll is tragic; typical of that toll is the boy dying in bewilderment and disbelief in the Rue du Bac.

But France remains nonetheless the cradle of the most valiant, the most humane and divine of the cultural, social and spiritual programs by which the unchanging Catholic ideals are translated into terms intelligible to each changing generation. If it be true that France has suffered greatly, physically and spiritually, at the hands of her scoundrels, it is also true that she is continually transfigured by the supernatural wisdom and the divine energies of her own sons and daughters among the saints. No criticism of contemporary France is worthy of our notice which fails to take into consideration the Sisters and the Catholic bookstores in the Rue du Bac as well as the bewildered agnostic boy who died there.

Only against the background of these two sets of facts—the sad history of how France has become de-Christianized and the glorious history of her Catholic revival in each generation—can one grasp the true significance of the work and words of the late Cardinal Suhard. No one will understand the extraordinary interest in the Cardinal's pastorals and other pronouncements throughout post-war France unless he is aware of how the Holy Spirit finds eager and ardent response at all times and places in France. No one will understand the emphasis and the overtones of the Cardinal's teaching unless he has some idea of how far advanced was the work of Satan in the nation to which Suhard addressed himself.

Some of the techniques by which the Cardinal sought to re-Christianize the paganized areas of life in his diocese have been the object of classroom criticism and round-table debate among a few theologians and critics of the French scene. Quite possibly a few of the programs which he sponsored and emphases which he stressed were ill-advised, though the time for the final word is hardly yet. This much is certain: all of them were part of the effort of a mighty man of God to bring back to the Holy Catholic Church a people whose best genius has always flourished in happy communion with that Church.

Even if some few of the many apostolic programs of the Cardinal disappointed his own high hopes, the impact of his teaching, particularly through the medium of his exalted pastorals, has been wide and mighty. The encyclicals of the modern popes have been cited as evidence of the clear operation of the Holy Spirit in our generation. The pastorals of Cardinal Suhard are certainly warm with the same divine fire and have given the apostolic witness within a nation (and indirectly beyond) which the Holy See has given before all the world.

The de-Christianized community which confronted the late Cardinal of Paris and which called out to everything that was Christlike in his apostolic mind and heart is not so peculiarly French in either its origins or its developments that any of us can consider it with detachment and complacency. The boy in the Rue du Bac is a type of France's tragedy and of a particular

INTRODUCTION

moment in her history; but he is not exclusively French. *Res nostra agitur:* the evils which have befallen one great Christian nation are not without their roots and unwholesome flower even in fields close to our homes, cities and sanctuaries. Secularism here is inevitably destined to produce a parallel to the paganism there. We can only pray that the counteracting apostolic vision and spiritual energy among us will be anywhere near as powerful as they are proving to be among the French.

We do well, therefore, to read the writings of Cardinal Suhard with great care and searching, not only because they record lofty moments in the Catholic French resistance to modern paganism, but also because they shed abundant light by which we in America can chart our course whenever and wherever Godlessness may seek to detour the progress of the Church among us. The time of our testing is bound to come; many of us think it is closer than any of us would wish. When it comes we shall undoubtedly be found to have been blessed by God with Suhards in our own hierarchy and with apostolic souls in our laity; such is the mercy of God. But it will also be good if we have profited from the wisdom of France's great champion of the faith in the face of paganism; that we can so learn is one of the blessings of the communion of saints as it operates on earth in the Holy Catholic Church.

The zealous scholars who have translated these works of Cardinal Suhard into English have paid the Church in France an affectionate tribute of gratitude and friendship by their work; at the same time, they have done the Church in America and the English speaking world an apostolic favor for which they deserve high praise and prayerful thanks.

✢ *John Wright*
Bishop of Worcester

THE MEANING OF GOD

Transcendence and Immanence are also two notions in the theology of God. In our pre-occupation with the brotherly aspect of the Son of Man we dare not lose the mystery of the Son of God. To forget that God created the world out of love and saved it out of love would be to lose the meaning of man and of God.

Contents

Page	
21	I. THE ABSENCE OF GOD
21	IN CONTEMPORARY SOCIETY
23	THE ATTITUDE OF CHRISTIANS
30	THE CHOICE BEFORE CHRISTIANS
35	II. THE TRUE GOD
36	THE MOST HIGH GOD
41	GOD WITH US
43	IN THE UNITY OF GOD
47	III. THE RETURN TO GOD
47	IN FAITH
53	IN ACTION
57	TWO TRUTHS TO BE REMEMBERED

The Meaning of God

I. THE ABSENCE OF GOD

The contemporary world has been often defined as the age of the machine and the age in which everything is relative; but the civilization of the present day can be defined more accurately by a feature which marks it off from any civilization which has preceded it. It is an age without God.

IN CONTEMPORARY SOCIETY

This absence of God causes contempt today among the most diverse kinds of men. It is not an evil on the surface of life; nor is it a geographical absence, as though God were missing from certain regions only. It is a chronic and universal absence, at one and the same time a fact and a deliberate intention. God is absent, banished, expelled from the very heart of life. Society has closed up on that exclusion and the resulting emptiness, a desert without God, is a void from which it is dying.

It would take a book, not merely a letter, if we were to try to enumerate all the forms of contemporary atheism. It is enough to realize this if we look at the posters in the streets, the pictures in magazines, the headlines in the press, the publicity given to certain films and novels. Nor could we hope to carry out such an analysis in a few pages, as much qualification would be needed.

We are concerned more with making Catholics realize this absence of God acutely and even painfully than with enumerating its different aspects. We must escape the slow movement of asphyxiation, and the need is urgent, by one of indignation. "God is absent from the towns, the countryside, laws . . . manners . . . art. He is absent even from the life of religion in the sense that those who still wish to be his friends do not need his presence." [1]

This last assertion may cause surprise. But need we be surprised if this universal atheism affects Christians themselves? Because they have to breathe that atmosphere they are in the end impregnated by it. The subtle poison is drawn in through

[1] Léon Bloy.

all the senses, the deadly peril being that it does not kill its victims but immunizes them against itself. Thus we do not have to go far to find the godless. They are found at every step. A large number of baptized Christians, while they are not genuine atheists, in practice live and act like atheists.

The Nominal Catholics

The first group among them is made up of the nominal Catholics, who only go to Church on big feasts. Can they really be said to know the meaning of God? They do indeed perform religious acts at certain times of the year, through family ties or because such acts are traditional; but can they really be said to have the faith? Is not their religious life an empty formalism? That this is so is shown by their conduct—it is no different from that of the unbelievers around them. They read the same books, patronize the same amusements, share the same judgments on life and events. But it is above all in their family life that the poverty of their religion appears. In relation to divorce, free unions, abortion, and birth prevention they are almost incredibly indulgent when they do not actively sponsor these doctrines. If this judgment be thought severe, think of the education parents of this kind are liable to give their children. Every day, even in the poorest homes, the greatest efforts are most touchingly made to obtain for the children everything they need: but only for the body. Health and hygiene have become idols to which everything else is sacrificed. All that relates to the formation of a Christian—conscience, religious faith, spirit of sacrifice, apostolate—is unknown or even despised. In the opinions of parents such things are superfluous. We need not be surprised therefore when adolescents systematically left to themselves on the plea of unshackled freedom swell the rising tide of juvenile delinquency or at the very least lead purely material lives, the end of which in their eyes and in those of their parents is death, beyond which there is nothing. How many baptized Christians weep over a grave "like those who have no hope"?

THE MEANING OF GOD

Practicing Catholics

Although they do not go to this degree of complete materialism, practicing Catholics themselves have also seriously lost the meaning of God. Sunday Mass and often the reception of the sacraments are for them a routine with which they are content and in which they settle themselves as in some privilege. Religion is for them an insurance against risk, a certificate of good education. Its obligations are performed as though they were a boring but necessary formality to which sacrifices must be made, just as sacrifices are made to other social conventions. Moral judgments are doubtless stricter and conduct more frequently inspired by duty. But what becomes of God in all this? It would be unjust to say that he is utterly forgotten; many belong to him more than they think or lead us to imagine. Their faith is awakened at intervals by some great happening in the Church or by some historical event. Nevertheless, in their lives as a whole God has ceased to be a personal God; he is a principle, a colorless abstraction. The awful and overwhelming words of Christ fall unheeded on their ears, the Gospel does not enter into their lives. Need we be surprised if the lives of so many Christians which proclaim Christ so slightly or so badly are barren or a scandal to the unbeliever?

THE ATTITUDE OF CHRISTIANS

Christians have felt this scandal painfully. Having begun to understand the meaning of the present crisis through a profound training in religion, they have chosen God and engaged themselves in the Church's service with a generosity admired in France and throughout the world.

Values Gained

For some twenty years—in practice since Catholic Action began—a magnificent effort has been made to bring the spirit of Christ into all the aspects of life. After a long period during which the Church was absent, some of the barriers between the contemporary world and the Christian tradition seem to have been lowered. A renewal of married and family life can be seen everywhere. Many young families show daily that an integral Christian life is possible in the ordinary conditions of life. In the field of education, among other successes it is enough to mention that of the Scouts. Boys who sought strength and the spirit of chivalry have been taught by this movement to find in union with Christ the impetus they needed to build up their personality. Thanks to specialized and general Catholic Action and especially to the Young Christian Workers a genuine and authentic spirituality of work now animates the worker and the student. They know that the world will not be brought back to Christ and they themselves be sanctified if they turn away from their daily tasks. They spontaneously transpose this mystique to social and civic action, and that not merely in order to make certain that the Church shall live in society but in order to establish among all men a union which shall reproduce on earth the image of the City of God.

Philosophy and theology, far from being closed to the perspectives of humanism, whether in literature or in science, have made a noteworthy attempt to integrate more fully a number of values—history, the idea of progress and others. Lastly, in matters of evangelization, a big advance has been made with the promotion of the laity. There remains of course much routine and habits of exclusiveness which belong to another age. But an immense movement to renew all Catholic institutions and especially the parish can now be seen. It shows that a number of routine attachments are merely temporary hardenings which will in due course be taken in hand and remolded by the life which is reaching them from every side.

It can thus be seen that by these concerted efforts a vast field has been withdrawn from the profane and placed under the prompting of the Holy Spirit. "Everything is grace . . ."—these words may serve as the banner and the conclusion for a development the like of which has never been seen.

THE MEANING OF GOD

Values Forgotten

Without indulging in the morbid form of disparagement apparent for some time and very frequent among ourselves, let us loyally recognize none the less that a serious overhaul is necessary. We invite all our militant Catholics to make this examination of conscience, but this in no way affects the fact of their engagement. What we asked from them last year as one of the conditions essential to the Growth of the Church we repeat just as insistently this year. The world will be saved only if Christians are present in it. More than at any other moment in history they ought to animate existing institutions, foresee and provide the reforms which must come. It would thus be contrary to our deliberate intention for anyone to avail himself of the analysis we intend to make as justifying his destructive and sceptical outlook or culpable escapism. The critic who never acts easily avoids mistakes—mistakes only come from action.

Further, it is not always a question of actual errors; the loyal examination we ask you to make concerns possible dangers, tendencies, or lines of experiment just as much as what has been achieved.

In any case everything comes back to the central question: do we possess the meaning of God? In other words, do the paganising surroundings imperceptibly color us? Have we kept the notion of God sufficiently high and sufficiently pure? We are engaged in the temporal—is our engagement sufficiently situated in the perspectives of the faith?—for without them our reforms would be neither legitimate nor successful. Does the meaning of man eclipse in us the meaning of God? Is God for us always God?

A Weakened Belief

The first danger concerns the very notion of God. The accent is put on everything that brings Him near to man: God as Father rather than God as Master. He is "Our Father," but on earth rather than "in heaven," a good God rather than the Sovereign Judge. Of the Word of God we have especially retained the adjective "Incarnate," and Christ has become the Friend, the Confidant, the Elder Brother, the model of life for multitudes of souls. But his Sacred Humanity, which was wholly referred and absolutely faithful to the Father, the Lord who grafts us upon the intimate life of the Love of the Three Persons—all that takes second place. Our age has fortunately rediscovered the extraordinarily brotherly character of the Son of Man but misses the mystery of the Son of God. We regard the coming of God into the world as a prodigious event and point to his action in history as at once directing it and giving it meaning. But not to see beyond that role, to forget that God has raised man towards himself, comes near to making God a means for the service of the world rather than a Being sufficient to himself apart from us. In short, we keep the Immanence of God [2] and are in danger of forgetting his Transcendence.

The "Meaning of Man" . . .

What is happening? Without our realizing it the great systems of philosophy and the great currents in the modern world with which our intelligence and sensibilities are entangled, inevitably exercise a contagious influence and penetrate the very bases of our faith. All the time the "meaning of man" tends to take the place in us of "the meaning of God."

Scientific discovery is directing everything towards technical achievement and the domination of material forces, and in the battle against all forms of enslavement *homo faber* expels *homo sapiens* and any form of disinterested contemplation. At the same time as man's power over things increases so also do his liberty and his autonomy. Man has the knowledge and the power; he is self-sufficient and has become his own center of interest. The majority of the modern tendencies in philosophy lead to atheistic humanism; and this is an abuse. In former days the attacks of heresy were directed against a dogma; during the

[2] Even though this word was recently disputed we use it in the meaning given to it in contemporary writing and in connection with the ideas of St. Thomas, expressed for instance in the title he gives to question 8 of *The Existence of God in All Things.*

THE MEANING OF GOD

last century they envisaged all dogmas. But at the same time a certain deism was still tolerated. Today the denial is the most radical of all, for the besetting sin of the modern age, as it was in the Old Testament, is idolatry, the idolatry of man.

... Has taken the Place of the Meaning of God

This conclusion clearly applies to the atheist; it applies also in a lesser but more subtle degree to the children of light themselves, for whom concentration upon man threatens to become a fatal poison. It consists in a reversal of values, in grafting God on man and not man on God. "What interests us is not God as he is in himself, but man, the world and its explanation, an answer to which must be found. Once the explanation has been given there is no need to look further . . . We have ceased to be aware of God in himself but only of God in us, that is of ourselves in our relation with God."[3] Everything is done as though God were at the service of man, as though he had a part to fulfill in relation to man, namely, the perfecting of the individual or of society.

Such a reversal of viewpoints, if it were once accepted, would destroy all religion. It would also contradict the whole of Scripture as well as the tradition of the Fathers and the Doctors of the Church. God made to our size, God in this human form, would cease to be God.

Lest these conclusions be thought to be too theoretical we will examine various aspects of contemporary Christian life; it will be seen to what lengths in tangible consequences this latent danger leads.

Contemplation is Misunderstood

The first consequence appears in the life of religion itself. Prayer of adoration and praise is little appreciated because the value of the virtue of religion and of the philosophical virtues is admitted only grudgingly. In some cases faith rather easily appears as no different from the contemporary idealistic systems by which their followers pledge themselves to a completely

[3] H. Paissac, "L'Athéisme des Chrétiens," supplement to "La Vie Spirituelle, May 15th, 1947.

human cause. Christians are aware of God in themselves but "they shrink from thinking of him in himself as though the question were unreal."[4] The prayer of contemplation is willingly reserved to religious as their special province, while the laity find God everywhere since he is immanent in the world.

The Sacred is Forgotten

It thus happens that sacramental and liturgical life suffer since their mystery is reduced. Because the only aspect seen of God is his familiar aspect, the sense of the Sacred has been lost. The pastoral clergy and chaplains unanimously find that one consequence is a weakening of the sense of sin along with an attendant distaste for the sacrament of Penance. Even among the best the feeling of guilt attaching to sin and the necessity of contrition in order to repair an ingratitude to God have become overlaid; we are close to ranking humility with natural moderation, purity with hygiene, charity with philanthropy. The expansive phrase is often repeated, and rightly, *sacramenta propter homines*. But it is not sufficiently realized that if the reception of the sacraments must always be made possible to the faithful, the reason is that they can thus the better appropriate them and be carried along in the great movement of praise and thanksgiving rising from this earth to God through His Son. If the sacraments are emptied of this essential content they will soon become lifeless rites.

The same is true of the Priesthood. Because some are tempted to make the priest the same as the militant—the best, it is true, and the most thoroughly committed—his particular function in the offering of the Sacrifice is no longer properly understood, with the result that the part played by the community is emphasized onesidedly. Is not the crisis in religious vocations due in part at least to this, that perhaps a plus value has been given to marriage (the high dignity of which can never be sufficiently stressed) while at the same time the consecration of the priest or religious is insufficiently emphasized and celibacy is not properly viewed as choosing God alone?

[4] H. Paissac, *op. cit.*

THE MEANING OF GOD

The Mystery of the Liturgy is Lost

This wrong idea of the minister of God is in reality nothing else but one aspect among others not infrequently met with of how the sense of the sacred in the liturgy has been lost. If the liturgy fortunately no longer keeps the laity as strangers to the wealth of the Church's official texts and gestures, it is on the other hand sometimes emptied of the essential element of mystery which has been sometimes excluded from too many ceremonies. The whole congregation making the Mass a dialogue is a real progress, just as long as too many mediocre commentaries, by destroying the silence, above all during the Canon of the Mass, do not intrude on too many of the faithful.

"Active" Holiness

The loss of the meaning of God is shown secondly in action, which tends to assert itself not only over contemplation but over sacrifice. Holiness is sometimes regarded as a beautiful flowering of humanism or the ultimate unfolding of the personality. In reaction to the negative moralism which was the vogue recently, the range of the active virtues is what is now offered to the young believer. To avoid formalism all spiritual constraint and often asceticism are condemned, for the reason that love covers everything and is everywhere sufficient. The primacy of charity was never before asserted as strongly as it is today, often enough because St. Augustine's *ama et fac quod vis* is interpreted too widely.

In fine, mortification—and even more readily obedience—are confined to those in religion, for the Hierarchy has become a stumbling block to many of the laity. Instead of seeing in the Hierarchy the emanation and the astounding prolongation in time of the mystery and the very person of Christ, they now see only the machinery of a complicated administration. It is not surprising therefore if a reckoning is demanded of an authority which is conceived as being built on merely human lines. Instead of seeing God they merely see man.

30 THE MEANING OF GOD

Success the Criterion

It is to be feared that in their determination to save all men, their brothers and especially those furtherest from them, Christians who are admirable indeed in generosity may fall into one of the dangers of our time, namely activism. What matters, what comes first, is action, and the dividend received; while the gratuitous gesture, the "useless" service from which nothing can be expected "historically" is looked down on and the profound value of failure is rarely understood. People are tempted to make another principle, the criterion "does it work," the matter of the apostolate, when the latter ought to be a disinterested communication of the integral message of the gospel. This is easily explained in an industrial age such as our own, in which everything is weighed, everything counted, everything measured, and belief is wrung from the mind by repeated publicity and propaganda. It is quite natural for such an influence to extend to the world of souls and for the messengers of Christ to be tempted to employ methods and even techniques which succeed. Do not many rely more on their own powers than on grace? And does not the lowered understanding of the sacraments everywhere noticeable derive from that? Natural methods are often preferred to the incomparable spiritual means, Penance and the Eucharist; and this is a new proof which cannot be gainsaid that even among the best there is a weakened sense of God.

THE CHOICE BEFORE CHRISTIANS

This somewhat long analysis has only touched on one or two of the main features in contemporary religious life; but it makes one thing quite plain: such deviations, which we warn the faithful exist and are possible dangers, have well known and interchangeable names: naturalism, pragmatism, subjectivism, secularism, and the like. That is no mere coincidence; there is a chain of cause and effect. The systems just mentioned, when they spread in the West, did not afterwards become extinct; they left behind them seeds which grew in the free at-

THE MEANING OF GOD

mosphere of the unbelieving world and in an underground but no less real manner in the Christian world.

From Philosophy . . .

In each of these worlds the systems mentioned were united by one common feature: they all had a philosophy of man. This philosophy, understood in two different ways, has divided contemporary thought into two distinct streams.

One, of optimism, believes that the indefinite progress of the universe by technical achievement due to an inherent law of dialectics will result in absolute happiness for humanity. The first duty is thus to believe in the future, to advance, to dedicate oneself unreservedly to the possession of the world.

A second broad current, the opposite of the first, moves towards pessimism. Everything is brought back to man considered in his concrete existence as a free being. But that existence, since it has no reason which explains it, is absurd, has no given direction, no meaning; and of this the actual bankruptcy of science and of civilization is sufficient proof. The attitude men must take is thus not a confident forward movement towards a better future but a conscious and despairing leap into nothingness.

. . . to Theology

Whether by effect or by coincidence, the minds of Christians deeply involved in the movement of the world hover between these two extremes, but on a different plane. They also can be summarily divided into two tendencies, or rather in both conscience is challenged by a different alternative. We exposed this dilemma a year ago in the measure that it affects Catholics in the matter of the Church. Confronted by the modern world what should be the Church's attitude: rupture or adaptation?

The problem thus appears here once more, but enlarged and more essential because it raises the whole question of humanism as well as the whole question of God. How much room does the meaning of God leave for the meaning of man? What rights does the kingdom of God leave for the city of man?

Transcendence or Separation?

At one extreme are those for whom they leave nothing. This world of ours must not only not be pursued for itself but we must not try to make it better or transform it. It is corrupt beyond redemption, an evil world, a closed system, the plaything of the dialectics of history and of technical change, and thus it admits of no "conversion." The world and grace are two different planes which call for divorce and not for reconciliation. The duty of the Christian is not to shape events or structures but to witness to the transcendence and the eternity of God, even to scandal.

This theoretical position is really based on two facts. Its followers point first of all to the many deviations we have just mentioned in the religious life of the present day and conclude that humanism has failed spiritually: it is an obstacle between the soul and God. To attempt to put God into the world is a hopeless task, the eternal temptation of making heaven on earth, the sin of idolatry. There is one way only of escaping from it, namely to return to a transcendental outlook and to find asylum unconditionally in the mystery of a sovereign and absolute Being compared with whom any interest taken in the things of this world is necessarily missing the point and procrastination.

In the present distress of the world is not this precisely what is revealed by the unconquerable instinct impelling man to seek outside himself the achievements larger than himself which he needs? With the unbeliever this instinct emerges in obscure substitutes for God, entities touchingly and defiantly deified such as Fraternity, Progress, Peace, Humanity; all of them impersonal substitutes for the God they do not know and think they do not seek. Next, how can we explain the extraordinary fascination now obvious among many Catholics for some Eastern religions except because they find in them a sense of the absolute and of divine contemplation which Western Christianity, too geared to natural methods, does not, they think, give them to the same degree?

But it is not merely in the attraction of Hinduism and

Theosophy that the need for a return to transcendence is shown; it is found in the Church itself. Among the faithful, opinion is on the watch for fresh apparitions and mystical phenomena. The appetite for manifestations of the supernatural and the deliberate absence of a critical sense in their acceptance, in contrast with the rightful prudence of the *magisterium*, is proof enough that many souls experience a hunger which a too human Christianity no longer satisfies.

. . . Or Immanence and Incarnation?

Against this exalted idealism and a supernatural position which looks elsewhere, the upholders of Immanence bring forward the great fact of the Incarnation. If God has sent his Son into the world and made him the model of the perfect man, he intended thereby to show us the road to follow, namely that we must reach God through man, through the holy humanity the Word assumed. If he shed his blood on earth, how is it possible short of blasphemy not to maintain that he did so except to redeem it? Ought not the efforts of the disciple of Christ be efforts in the world, in order to complete the Redemption done by its Head?

Even those however who have chosen to engage themselves in the temporal (and we remind you here, without repeating the reasons we have already given, that this is a pressing duty for every Christian) are anxious. For they know only too well that those attempting to complete creation—to "increase and possess the earth"—and to organize the world to the image of the Kingdom of heaven are in danger of becoming so enamoured of their task that they may forget the other city which it ought to mirror and towards which it should lead. A degradation of values is thus caused whereby what is specifically Christion loses its savour and disappears. The spirit of the apostolate can become proselytism or recruitment, charity can become philanthropy or party comradeship, hope merely trust in the indefinite possibility of progress; faith in man deprives man of that in him which makes his genuine nobility, namely, that he is incapable of completing himself except by going beyond the possibilities within him and by embracing vistas larger than his own.

There is undoubtedly no more cruel disillusionment for a Christian or for a movement a more searing failure than the hackneyed experience countless times repeated in the past: the apostle sets out with enthusiasm, the carrier of the Good News; he knows that a long road stretches ahead of him before he can come up with the shepherdless masses, that prejudices have to be overcome, aspirations shared, a destiny to be shouldered in common. And when the long effort has been accomplished and he has made his way into the heart of the problem, when contact is re-established and he feels he is quite close to those he sought and similar to them . . . he suddenly finds himself with nothing to give. The message he bore has grown dim and the treasure scattered. The apostle has done the opposite of what the merchant did in the gospel, when he sold all he had in order to obtain the pearl without price;[5] he has let the divine treasure slip through his fingers and all he now has to offer are human things. He may be utterly devoted and a friend to all—it is no use; for he is incapable of satisfying the expectations of those he hoped to save. For "man cannot live by bread alone,"[6] nor by improved conditions of living, nor by human affection. By whatever name he may call it, man's hunger is for God.

Return to the Doctrine of God

Those Catholics who are most deeply involved in action feel this acutely and are made anxious by it. Therefore we intend this year also to point out what road should be followed by those who are scrutinizing their conscience and loyally wonder which direction to take.

To those who rightly rebel against a naturalistic system which reduces God to our human measure and who therefore refuse to see him in this world, we wish to show that the Infinite Being is present to his creatures and relies on our labours for the world to be dedicated to him.

[5] Math., 13:45-46
[6] Math., 4:4.

THE MEANING OF GOD

To those on the other hand who are in danger of losing sight of the absolute transcendence of God in the eagerness of their engagement in the temporal, we point out that he who made himself one of us nevertheless remains apart from us and unique.

Only the theology of God, by showing that these two unilateral conceptions are complementary, will make their reconciliation possible, and only it will enable us to save the meaning of man by returning to the meaning of God. In the third section of this letter we will lay down the resolutions which should direct an impartial examination.

II. THE TRUE GOD

What are the sources from which we draw a proper knowledge of God? The Church formally says there are two, the first being reason, which proves to us that God exists and can moreover tell us something authentic about his nature although in a very summary fashion. The Vatican Council enlarges on this double power and duty of the human mind. "Whoever says that the one and only true God, our Creator and Lord, cannot be known with certainty by the natural light of the human reason by means of created things, let him be anathema." [1]

But in reality and by right such meagre knowledge yields place to an infinitely deeper and warmer knowledge, that of revelation. "God," says Pascal, "speaks well of God" but man does not. It is therefore in the bible that Christians will find what God teaches about himself, as well also as in tradition, in the writings of the *magisterium* and the Doctors of the Church, which form the complementary and living source of faith.

It need scarcely be said that in these pages it is not our intention to recall or even to sketch a treatise on God. Our purpose is to take some of these inspired texts and show that in them God appears constantly and at the same time in two aspects which are apparently contradictory: he is sometimes transcendent and apart, at others present to man and immanent in the world.

[1] Denz., 1806

THE MOST HIGH GOD

We advise all who feel hemmed in by a closed and stifling world to open the Old and the New Testaments. They will there find vistas which will liberate them, and the excellent food of the only true God.

The Mystery

The first element when we meet God will be that of mystery. God is the Inaccessible, and he is inaccessible for all. "No one has seen God," says St. John;[2] and even for those to whom God gives himself to be known he remains the hidden God. "Show me thy face, that I may know thee," asked Moses, only to receive the categorical answer: "Thou canst not see my face: for man shall not see me and live."[3] No illusion is therefore possible: God remains the incomprehensible, and the human mind possesses no key which can unlock his secret. All that the human mind at its best can experience is fear and consternation at the impenetrable mystery. Of God man knows that he does not understand him, and that all he sees of him is his shadow falling on the things of this world: he remains inaccessible, in his intimate reality, to the eyes of the spirit. "Verily Thou are a hidden God."[4] "We realize how majestic the nature of God is," says St. Gregory of Nyssa, "not by understanding it but because it cannot be proved by any demonstration or grasped by our intellectual powers,"[5] and St. Augustine insists just as much: "God is not what you imagine or what you think you understand. If you understand you have failed." St. Thomas in his turn does not try to feed our pretensions or our flippancy.[6] God is darkness. To know God is to realize that we do not know him.

---

[2] John, 1:18.
[3] Exodus, 33:13, 20.
[4] Isaias, 45:15.
[5] Greg. Nyss., *In Cant. hom.* 12.
[6] "Dicimus in fine cognitionis nostrae Deum tanquam ignotum cognoscere." (*In Boet. de Trinitate*, 1, 2; primum). God remains quite other: "Neque intelligitur, neque dicitur, neque nominatur, neque in aliquo ex-

Analogical Knowledge

This conclusion does not mean, as some philosophers maintain, that God cannot be known by reason; it merely makes clear that the created mind is too small to encompass and seize the Infinite Being. God is utterly beyond any ability of ours. Christian philosophy tells us that there are two ways of reaching him. The first and royal road consists in saying of God all that we know of created perfection and developing this to an infinite degree, and by extension to the nth degree to try and gain some idea of a perfection that is infinite and uncreated. We arrive at it by the principle of causality and analogy; and our knowledge of God is thus neither a myth, nor false, nor exhaustive; it is meagre and relative.

Negative Knowledge

But the mind has a second road to God, the way of negation, the opposite of the first. In order to be certain that we do not contradict the infinite, by bringing him within our categories, we deny of him all that we affirm of ourselves, and we define him by all that we ourselves are not.[7] The philosophers and the theologians, but especially the great spiritual writers, thus sought to know God by denying any common measure between his being and the world. "All the being of creatures is nothing when compared with the infinite being of God . . . Not one of them comes even close to God, or has any likeness to his being." [8] "There is not merely a difference of degree but of essence: I am who am, thou art who art not," our Lord said

---

istentium cognoscitur, omnia est, et in nullo nihil et in omnibus cunctis cognoscitur et ex nullo nulli." St. Thomas took these words and commented on them in his *Expositio super Dionysium de divinis nominibus*, c. 7, lectio IV.

[7] "The God of St. Thomas," says M. Gilson, "is even far more inaccessible than the God of Aristotle, who was quite inaccessible enough already. All we can situate is his metaphysical position without being at all able to conceive what he is, but only 'what he is not and the connections everything else has with him' (St. Thomas, contra Gen., I, 30)."—Gilson, *Le Thomisme*, p. 150.

[8] St. John of the Cross, *Ascent of Mt. Carmel*, I, 6.

to St. Catherine of Sienna. "Every created thing considered in itself is nothingness";[9] and St. John of the Cross goes even further: "the beauty, the grace and the attractiveness of creatures, when compared in their entirety with the beauty of God, are utterly ugly and horrible."

These phrases and many another are not rhetorical developments, nor are they condemnations of the work of our Creator; their whole aim is to isolate for us the absolute transcendence of God.

God is Holy

At the very moment God allows himself to be known to us, he remains separate, quite other from us. Between his immaculate pureness and man, infirm, weakened and sordid, the gulf cannot be bridged: "Come not nigh hither; put off the shoes from thy feet," God ordered Moses from the burning bush [10] for he is "the Holy One of Israel."[11] Respect and trembling are the sentiments which are least adapted to recognize his mystery.[12] Adoration is the inescapable condition always, even in heaven: "Holy, holy, holy is the Lord God, the Almighty."[13] Faced with God, the children of Adam know they are radically impure and are thereby unworthy to continue in life. God has no equal: "To whom then have you likened God? Or what image will you make for him?" he has himself asked.[14]

Sovereign

He is for this reason the Sovereign Lord: "I am the Lord, and there is none else: there is no God besides me,"[15] the Living God, self-sufficing, in no way bound to explain himself

[9] St. Thos., Ia IIae, 109, 2, 2.
[10] Exodus, 3:5.
[11] Isaias, 1:4.
[12] Yahweh was "feared" by Isaac: Gen., 31:53, Jacob "trembled," Gen., 28:16; cf. for the same meaning Heb., 10:34.
[13] Apoc., 5:8.
[14] Isaias, 40:18.
[15] Is., 45:5, 43:13; &c.

THE MEANING OF GOD

to us, to whom must go all obedience and all homage: "I am the Lord thy God, mighty, jealous." [16]

He is the master and free: his revelation erupts into the life of man and disturbs our established institutions. Abraham had to leave Ur of the Chaldees,[17] Moses to lead his people through the desert in spite of his attempt to avoid the task,[18] for God's interests take first place over ours. He has his plan and his ways are beyond our scrutiny. He is the master of time and of history; he manipulates both as he wishes: "for my thoughts are not your thoughts; nor your ways my ways." [19] This mastery of God over the development of the world is beyond the ability of man to grasp, for we look upon the events of time as we would wish them to be.

What is true of the Old Testament is true also of the New. "Mosaic and prophetic revelation was not destroyed, it was consummated in the gospel. The affirmation that God is one, that he is the sole Lord and loved above everything created, was to be as sacred to the Christian as much as and even more than it has been to the Jew." [20] Our Lord did not cease to point to the infinite majesty of his Father: "Why dost thou call me good? None is good, except God only." [21] His sovereignty was without division: "You are not to claim the title of Rabbi; you have but one Master, and you are all brethren alike. Nor are you to call any man on earth your father; you have but one Father, and he is in heaven." [22] Our Lord mystified his contemporaries as much as Yahweh had mystified their ancestors: Israel expected a victorious Messias and the Son of Man told them of the ruin of Jerusalem and of the Cross. The mystery of God's ways remains inscrutable to man: there also God is apart from man.[23]

[16] Exodus, 20:5.
[17] Gen., 12:1.
[18] Exodus, 4:13-14.
[19] Isaias, 60:8.
[20] P. Lebreton, *Lumen Christi*, p. 5.
[21] Mark, 10:18.
[22] Math., 23:7-8.
[23] The teaching of the Church is no less clear: "The Holy, Catholic, Apostolic, and Roman Church believes and confesses that there is one

The End of Humanism ...

Having reached this stage in his researches, it seems that the Christian has no need to choose; his road seems inexorably laid down; to divorce himself from the world and take refuge in transcendence, with the two consequences which are inevitable in relation to actual life, the end of humanism and the end of history. How should humanism be other than blasphemy when every created value is worthless and there is not merely an abyss but a contrast between the High God and the worthless dust we are? [24] How can any interest taken in this fleeting life be other than madness if our last end be considered, and an inexcusable frivolity with the eternal? How can man's attempt to constitute a human order not escape the charge of idolatry—that sin which more than any other calls down the anger of Yahweh? Since God is the great one apart, since he is not "immanent" in his creature, the latter cannot as such situate itself outside him without being against him. Whatever we do, the "meaning of man" goes directly against the "meaning of God," and the meaning of God is precisely the greast lesson and the constant reminder of the whole of the bible.

... and of History?

The same is true of history. Since God seems to despise "our ways" and bothers with them merely in order to upset the normal course of events by disconcerting interventions, we can no longer talk of the developments in time or of the progress

---

only true and living God, Creator and Lord of heaven and earth, all powerful, eternal, immense, incomprehensible, infinite in intelligence, in will and in every perfection who, being a unique spiritual substance by nature, absolutely simple and unchangeable, must be declared distinct from the world in fact and by essence, happy in himself and by himself, and lifted above all that is and can be conceived outside him."—Vat. Coun., const. Dei Filius, cap. 1.

[24] St. John of the Cross says so: "All the wisdom in the world and all human cleverness compared with the infinite wisdom of God is sheer and extreme ignorance. All the riches of the world and the glory of creation, compared with the wealth of God, are extreme and abject poverty."— Ascent of Mount Carmel, I, chap. 6.

THE MEANING OF GOD

of society and of human institutions. God does not act from within but from without, in a completely external way. He does not arrive from this side of things but from the other. An "eschatological" direction must therefore take the place of the views of history. Our Savior did not teach us to say "Our Father who are in our hearts" but "Our Father who art in heaven," and it is there and not here that we must look for him and find him in pure faith and contempt of the world.

GOD WITH US

But is this notion of God complete? He is apart. But is he not also the everywhere present? Scripture and tradition with equal certainty show this second aspect of God. He wished also to be God with us, a God who gives himself.

The Two Alliances

The revelation of this began in the Old Testament with the idea of an alliance,[25] which lays down from the beginning and with growing clearness that God is not only a mystery of infinity but a mystery of love. He calls Israel, then all the nations, to community with him, first in the imperfect reconciliation made by the first "testament," then in the pardon and the intimate union of the new alliance in Jesus Christ. What else do the prophets proclaim if not the rigorous and tender love of "the God of Israel"?[26] Because if God seems to deny or upset history, this is not the contempt or the cruel game of a despot, but a tireless appeal to us to enlarge our vision.

He intervenes from without in order to transfigure us from within. Abraham had to leave his own country, but it was in order that he might become the father of those who believe; Moses had to obey even against his own will, but it was in order to save a people; St. Paul was thrown to the ground on the Damascus road, but it was in order to become the apostle of the Gentiles. God uses men and events to fulfil his plan of

[25] Gen., 17:1; Exodus, 32:10.
[26] Cf. Isaias, 43:4; 49:10; cf. also the words of Jeremias in the Office of the Sacred Heart.

salvation. Can we say after this that he does not lead history? Will anyone say that the God Apart is not also everywhere present?

Everywhere Present

But this presence of God in its turn is merely a particular case of a more universal fact and intention, that God, by the fact of their creation, should be present in all creatures. "In Him we live, move and have our being," says St. Paul.[27] In some splendid pages of the *Summa*, St. Thomas takes up this statement of "God existing in things."[28] "As long as a thing has being, God must be present in it . . . it is a necessary conclusion from this that God is in all things and in an intimate way."[29]

What reason teaches on this matter is exactly what is taught by scripture: not pantheism, not the God of Aristotle wholly apart from a world he does not know. "The God of the Christians," writes Pope Pius XII, "is not an empty phrase . . . or an abstract idea decked out by thinkers. He transcends all that is, and everything that exists owes its existence to him . . . millions of men can hurry through the streets . . . absorbed by their affairs . . . without ever thinking of God. Yet it is he who keeps them in existence."[30]

What then must we say of God's presence by grace in the soul, a presence which is not merely that of God the Creator immanent in his creature, but the intimacy of the three divine

---

[27] Acts, 17:28.

[28] Ia., Q.8, a.1.

[29] "Our very being," says P. Sertillanges, "bathes in the being of God, who is the being of our being, if such an expression may be allowed; and there is immanence . . . On the other hand, St. Thomas again says: 'God is incomparably lifted above every form of being' and there is his transcendence. What isolates God and makes him 'the Holy One' is the unique plenitude of God . . . This plenitude is also the reason why nothing can subsist except in him, a conceptual relationship we express by the term 'immanence' or more currently by 'God being present in all things.' "—Sertillanges, *Dieu ou Rien?*: pp. 87-88.

[30] Pius XII, in a radio message to the United States Catechetical Congress.
Documentation Catholique, December 8th, 1946.

THE MEANING OF GOD

persons shared with us? "We will come and make our dwelling there." [31] The last word has been spoken, the very mystery made open to us: "God," says St. John, "is love." At once the double chasm is bridged; God's sovereignty is now seen to be love, seeking its own glory by communicating itself. God in himself and God given to us are one, the holy God is also Emmanuel, God with us. If we forget that gigantic reality—which is also certain—we lose sight of the meaning of God and fall into a Manichean conception of the relations between God and the world.

IN THE UNITY OF GOD

Transcendence and immanence are thus the two notions which the theology of God reveals to us and tells us never to separate. God is simple; but our minds are so made for understanding the world that they cannot imagine what the infinite is except by its relations with the finite, within or without, immanent or transcendent. A believer may try hard to convince himself of the shortcomings of his intelligence when confronted with the Absolute, and of the truth these two aspects simultaneously contain; but all he can do to express these opposites is to set them down side by side. The danger thereupon is great of retaining only one of the two terms: of seeing God only as opposite from the world, with the conclusion going with it that he must have nothing to do with the fatal and corrupt dialectic of this life; or on the contrary, of not seeing God except in the world and in life, with the danger of divinising one or the other. In each case the result is secularism: God in the world or the world in God, each being the end of two distinct processes.

Those who hold uncontaminated transcendence do indeed see the majesty of God but they at once contradict it and injure it by limiting it; for they withdraw it from creation, mistake the rule of providence over the world, and are quite blind to the fact of incarnation. At once, quite naturally, they tend in practice to isolation, to faith without works, to contemplation without the apostolate, to the Church deprived of her features

[31] John, 14:23.

in time. That attitude of refusal is the same which, according to the period and the problem, is called Quietism, Pessimism or Jansenism.

On the other side those who uphold an exclusive immanence forget the infinity of God. Their wish to put God everywhere ends in withdrawing him from everything; for what remains of a God who is present only in the world, a God who has ceased to be present to himself, a God who is no longer God? What meaning is there in an immanence which is the immanence of no one or of nothing? Incarnation pre-supposes being, and in the same way immanence postulates continuing existence and continuing self-sufficiency. It has been pointed out that the wish to humanize God in order to make him closer to man is an error; God is close only if he is the High God; and far from denying transcendence, immanence all the time supposes it. Without it the world, far from being intelligible, is absurd, inexplicable or guilty; inexplicable because it has no object, absurd because it has no reason for being, guilty because it sets itself up in competition with "him apart from whom there is no God." [82] We can indeed get rid of the problem by confusing God with the world, and at once the result is pantheism.

In Incarnate Love

We once more find that the truth lies in uniting and harmonizing these two symmetrical statements. The God of Israel has the right to be called "the true God" because, combining all perfections, he is both pure spirit and creator, him of whom it can be said "True praise of thee is silence," and "All ye works of the Lord, bless the Lord." [83] The problem is not solved by an abstract formula; the solution itself is alive and is found in a person, the Word of God. He is revealed to us by the Incarnation, "taking the nature of a slave," [84] come among men, at the same time the equal of the Father by his nature as God. The God of the philosophers is thus outstripped in grandeur, and that of the philanthropists in nearness to man.

---

[82] Isaias, 45: 5.
[83] Canticle of the Three Young Men.
[84] Philip., 2:7.

THE MEANING OF GOD

The Lord we adore is not a compromise of two extremes, but the completing of both in the mystery of his person.[35] Here again, and especially here, everything is unified and made perfect in love. Everything is explained by him . . .

Gratuitously Given

. . . on condition that this statement is at once clarified. The expression "synthesis" and "unity" in God of the two words making up transcendence—immanence is capable of being wrongly understood and of giving the impression that they are on the same plane, that they are two complementary perfections inherent in the essence of God. It is quite clear that this is not true. Immanence is understood only of God's presence to created beings. Created beings, however, are not necessary beings; creation is the consequence of a free act in God, is not part of his nature, and adds nothing to him.[36] God continues independently of the world with his infinite perfections. The brief analysis just made from the bible and theology applies to a state of fact only, to a reality which is, but might not have been, or might have been different.

All the perspective which the meaning of an incarnate God causes to faith and humanism are admissable only in the hypothesis of the economy of salvation, which revelation presents to us as a fact. To forget that, to forget that God created the world freely and out of love, and that he also saved it by the same means by becoming incarnate out of love, would be to lose the meaning of man and the meaning of God.

Meaning of God, and Meaning of Man

Both are bound up together, not by their depending upon each other, for God suffices to himself, and immanence and

---

[35] St. Hilary thus describes God: "*Deus, totus intra extraque, supereminens internus, circumfusus et infusus,*" a double aspect of God much insisted on by the Fathers.

[36] It has been pointed out that St. Albert the Great, in an obviously expanded sense, calls the world "*accidens Dei,* an accident of God," meaning by this that the world is not essential to God but that he is essential to it, as substance is essential to accident and is part of the definition of accident.—Sertillanges, *Dieu ou Rien?* p. 87.

incarnation on his side are love absolutely and freely given; but in the sense that in its definition humanism is entirely dependent on the idea of God.

If God is only immanent, the consequence is pagan humanism; man is enclosed within himself, a prisoner in the world, and for ever incapable of going beyond himself.

If God is only transcendent, the world loses all meaning, ceases to be related to the mind and the heart, becomes night and sin; man becomes a prey to an unappeasable disquiet.

Condemnation of Humanism

But if God is "he who is," a High God as well as a near God, everything is different, and humanism is provided with two foundations.

The first comes from the fact of creation. To pledge oneself to action in the world is justified, because everything being upheld by the presence of God in everything, bears the imprint of the creator. That presence and likeness exist more deeply in man, since in virtue of his spiritual nature he has been created to the image of God. But God is present in things not merely to preserve them in existence; by pure love he decided to become incarnate in the person of his Son. This second degree of immanence draws God closer to man, and thereby the world and mankind are consecrated.

Thus by divine adoption in Christ man assumes an infinitely higher likeness to God, for God places in him by his grace his living imprint.

By this double title—man as citizen of this earth and son of God—the whole of Christian humanism is founded, and with that our temporal and supernatural engagement is entirely justified. On the one hand, man can and ought to root himself in the world, following the example of its Head; and that is a reason for his nobility. On the other hand, he is called to go infinitely beyond his own nature, and he already shares in the kingdom of Heaven: *Conversatio nostra in coelis est:* our true home is in heaven.[37]

The humanism of the Christian is thus founded in its whole

[37] Philip., 3:20.

extent, since it comes from the only lasting origin, that is, from God. The conclusion is crucial, and it does not appear as a new problem, but as the only solution for the theoretical and practical lack of certainty dividing Christians in the problem of their attitude towards the world. It is not a question, it need hardly be said, of exhausting here or even setting out the scheme of the vast problem of humanism. Others are busy in this matter, philosophers, theologians and saints, for it is one of the most urgent problems of our day. We cannot emphasize enough how urgent and fruitful such an examination is if it remains closely faithful to itself and docile to the suggestions of the Church's *magisterium*. Our only object, in the same spirit in which we write our pastoral letter, *Growth or Decline?* and in order to enrich from within the lines of action we then gave you, is to show that the meaning of God can alone safeguard the primacy of the spiritual and make legitimate and efficacious a wholehearted engagement in the temporal.

III. THE RETURN TO GOD

We are now able, in no arbitrary fashion, to see the ways this return to God must take; it is urgent and indispensable if the hesitations of Christians committed to action are to be resolved. The remedy is not far to seek, nor need we call everything in question and turn away from action. On the contrary, we cannot emphasize strongly enough the degree to which the methodical efforts of priests and militants are shown to be indispensable. It would be superfluous to insist upon a truth so evident and so often preached in recent years by the Holy See. We ask you to be more faithful than ever to your engagement in the spiritual order and the temporal order, as we invited you a year ago. There is a hierarchy of values to be saved, a spirit to be breathed into what we think and do.

IN FAITH

We must go to the root of the trouble, that is, the weakening of belief; as we pointed out at the beginning, this is the feature found in all contemporary errors.

Belief

Many who believe are convinced that they have the faith. In fact the God they honor is often a God created or modified by themselves. They do not accept, they choose they do not receive revelation, they elaborate a rational divinity, a dangerous counterfeit, a product of their own guilty errors.[1] God, we have seen, in Mystery, and his infinite being, escapes our grasp. The Absolute does not become known to us as the conclusion to a syllogism or as a clear and distinct idea. We shall only reach him by faith. That knowledge is certain knowledge because it is enlightened by love; but it will always remain obscure. The infinite is beyond our human experience; and the ineffable reality of a trinitarian God is larger than any gesture or intuition we can make.

Must we therefore refuse to use our reason?

The whole effort made by theology is a standing witness to the contrary. Its rational elaboration does not start with man; it starts with revelation and stands on the authority of God. We do not therefore deduce God from history or from man, we receive him as what he is, prodigious and free, as the Reality without answer or precedent.

The world and human life in this perspective are explained. "I am the First and the Last."[2] "I am Alpha, I am Omega, the beginning of all things and their end."[3]

It is not he who is at our service but we who ought to gravitate towards him as our lifegiving end. This straightforward reversal of direction eliminates any anthropomorphism from religious life and centres it truly on God by a surrender of self which is both respectful and disinterested. Where before we were sensitive to our rights we become receptive to the idea that we have duties to God.

This is not a matter of a mere verbal quibble or a sheer

[1] "Above all beings there is the unique being, God . . . It is not man's belief in God which makes God exist; it is because God exists that all men, if they do not deliberately close their eyes to the truth, believe in him and address their prayers to him."—Pius XII, *divini Redemptoris*.

[2] Isaias, 48:12.

[3] Apoc., 1:8.

THE MEANING OF GOD

mental exercise. Very real questions are involved and at once illuminated. Take Sunday as an example; for the majority of Christians it is undoubtedly a day of rest and rightly so. But for how many is this rest really concerned with God? Who among them, when they have once been to Mass, still feel that they continue to be involved in the Lord's day, a day which belongs supremely to him, a day which in the long continued story of our lives and cares he has reserved to himself in order that we shall turn to him in prayer, peace and praise?

Prayer

The return to God must show itself most clearly by prayer.

We do indeed pray today, but we pray far too much for ourselves. Perhaps we also pray far too much for others, and then our prayer for them is spoilt by interest or takes the place of thanksgiving and praise. We must become conscious again of the grandeur and splendor of God, annihilate ourselves before his majesty, humbly recognize our sinfulness before his countenance, dedicate all things to his exclusive love.

An effort needs to be made to restore the sense of the sacred, the progressive weakening of which has been pointed out by many competent judges, to the external manifestations of religious life. In our Father in Heaven we are tempted to see merely an easy-natured providence, and in his eternal Son a companion like ourselves. Let us therefore restore to the centre of our own lives that "fear of God" and respect for actions and feelings which, far from harming the descent and intimate presence of love in the soul, on the contrary fittingly translate how deeply conscious we are of our smallness.

Return to Mystery

The liturgical revival which can be seen so successfully at work today will then produce all its fruits and will not be jeopardized by the obsession, lawful in intention but sometimes clumsy in procedure, of adapting it to modern society. The liturgy will undoubtedly be able to carry further all the values which uplift life, and harmonize the linguistic, aesthetic and community methods which are clearly necessary if we are to draw all men into a truly Catholic worship. There is no question of returning to the pernicious individualism which dried up so many generations; we must continue more than ever to promote a community worship. But we must not be afraid to bring silence into it, a silence which is not the collective dumbness of individual worshippers but a community silence which unites all as brothers and lifts the soul to God.

Contemplation

This collective prayer which is so productive of good ought however to be always accompanied by or rather express a more profound and more secret intercourse with God. All prayer is not on the same plane. The best prayer is the prayer of which our Lord said: "When thou art praying, go into thy inner room and shut the door upon thyself, and so pray to thy Father in secret." [4] A disciple of Christ should be capable deliberately and alone of paying homage to God by shutting himself off from the world and forgetting himself in prayer.

It is at this point that the phrase which will liberate us must be spoken. Admittedly the word contemplation sometimes frightens us and seems to provoke contradiction; it at once evokes an idea of exceptional lives, ecstasies, apparitions and mystical phenomena which ordinary Christians attribute to a few privileged initiates. It is, on the other hand, patient of various meanings and is not without prestige among the intellectual elites which are attracted by the alluring systems of the East. The reason for this lies in mere appearances: through not drawing sufficiently deeply on the springs of Christian life men set out to find springs or evasions which are less pure, and on their return are less ready for the sacrifices of ordinary life. All contemplation must be kept separate from the weakened forms and unhealthy substitutes in which religious feeling and highbrow talk delude their authors and others.

Contemplation and Inner Life

Contemplation contains two realities each of which is different. The first, that of the contemplative separated from the

[4] Math.; 6:6.

THE MEANING OF GOD

world, is directed to keeping ever present and fresh the dialogue which united Christ to the Father in his long hours of prayer. The contemplative, indispensable to the Church, is dedicated by his state to witness to the transcendence of God. The duty of the Christian is to understand the contemplative; and that of the contemplative is to remain faithful to his mission.

But in ordinary language contemplation also means a reality more readily accessible; and it is to this form of it that we invite you. It is not necessary to be a theologian or a great mystic to reach it; it is enough to enter into oneself and approach God as a present and living person. It therefore consists above all in an effort of *direction:* instead of turning our prayer towards things and men it is enough to turn it towards God.

Face to Face with God

The essence of contemplation is to make God our object, to place ourselves face to face with him, to direct ourselves towards him, as a river runs to the sea instead of wasting its waters in the sand or harmfully spreading them beyond its banks. When we look at God, who has no equal, all we need do is let the soul admire and be uplifted by his grandeur and his beauty. It is enough to let the soul sing and to tell God that we thank him for all his goodness, to offer him our work, our joy, our sorrow, and above all ourselves. The essential thing is to become humble before him and to open ourselves to him, letting him invade the soul with his strength and gentleness. Contemplation is thus not a matter of human ingenuity; we make ourselves over without holding back, like children and time after time, to that inner grace ceaselessly at work upon us and uninterruptedly calling us to turn ourselves to God.

This invitation is addressed in the first place to priests. The Church for good reasons enjoins this upon them;[5] priests are not merely the leaders of Christian society—they are dedicated to revealing the mysteries of the love of God.

---

[5] Code of Canon Law, 125, 2; 595, 1-2; 1367, 1.

THE MEANING OF GOD

The Spiritual Effort to Be Made

The lives of the saints, however, show that this grace is not confined to the clergy.

With some, circumstances willed by providence favor a life of intimacy with God, and more than one solitary soul can contribute for his fellowmen a witness which is far more precious than direct apostolic work. No special state of life is necessary to be thus dedicated to Love; and there is no life which cannot and ought not set aside some time for prayer and for attention to God. Closed retreats and spiritual reading will help to unite these souls even more to their Father in Heaven.

Return to the Bible

The effort at contemplation we ask you to make is in practice and first of all a return to the main springs of our religion. Instead of stopping at the many secondary works and anaemic commentaries, the multiplication of which stands between us and the parent texts, let active Christians go to these texts and re-discover the bible. In reaction against the Protestant doctrine built on private interpretation, Catholics were long severed from the infinite riches contained in the word of God. Today that danger has disappeared and we are glad to recognize the movement which grows stronger every day in favour of the inspired books. Brought up in a scientific, technical and materialistic world intellectuals of the present day have ceased to find God in the old framework. They will return to God active in history by returning to the plan of redemption contained in the bible. We encourage this movement, with the precautions necessary for it to remain in the truth of the faith committed to the Church.[6] This spontaneous movement is, we think, providential; for nowhere except in the Prophets, in the

---

[6] We remind you that in these matters no one may read a bible printed without notes. An annotated edition contains explanations which are indispensable to the vast majority of Christians. The modern culture they have received has not familiarized them with the history of the Jewish people, or with the question of literary genres which is so necessary for an understanding of the bible.

Gospels, in St. Paul and in the Apocalypse shall we find a witness to the Grandeur and the Holiness of God.

The Sacraments

We must also return to the sacraments, if we wish, in contemplation, to nourish it and to remain in the path of logic; because if the sacraments exist for man they also exist, and in the first place, for God. They are there so that we may be invaded by them and by them be dedicated to God; and if the sacraments of Confirmation, Penance and the Eucharist are looked at in this way they will undoubtedly assume an absolutely new meaning, indeed their whole meaning, for all who, exacting in their demands upon religion, had failed to realize, through the absence of this view, the depth and the finality of the sacraments.

IN ACTION

Belief, adoration and contemplation, these are the primary elements in a return to the meaning of God; but they raise once again the problem of action. What becomes of action in a religious life apparently wholly occupied by the values of contemplation? Ought it to be tolerated? It is not a matter here of again questioning its theoretical value—on this we have sufficiently insisted; but many wonder how in practice these two forms of Christian life can be reconciled. Some wonder if Christian life and contemplative life are not necessarily in opposition or mutually harmful.

Primacy of Contemplation

One thing is certain: contemplation comes first by right and must come first in fact; for contemplation, that is the inner life is nothing else in man than the free and deliberate manifestation in us of God's own life, begun on this earth at the first Pentecost and in us on the day we were baptized. It is not limited to pious exercises but is to be identified with the living faith so frequently inculcated by the scriptures.[7] By it, and by

[7] "The just shall live in his faith." Hab., 2:4; Rom., 1:17; Heb., 10:38; Gal., 3:2.

the theological virtues of faith, hope and charity, man enters into communication with God present in it; and by them man's powers of action are mysteriously assumed into that stream of love which St. John uses to define God.[8] Inner life is the eruption of faith into all our powers, the unfolding of the state of grace and of the indwelling in us of the three divine persons; in short, the soul living under the motioning of the Holy Spirit.

What runs counter to contemplation may be called "activism," that is, procedures and systems applied externally which, because they are artificial, are for this reason bound to fail. But it is not action,[9] for action is merely the external manifestation or overflow of a superabundant life of faith and love, a thin screen pierced by the light of God. "The Holy Spirit, shining in those from whom all stain has been purified, makes them spiritual by contact with himself. Similarly, just as transparent substances, when subjected to light, themselves glitter and give off light, so does the soul, illuminated by the Holy Spirt, give light to others and itself become spiritual." [10]

Contemplation and Apostolate

Far from being enemies, action and inner life thus complete each other and mutually continue each other.

A return, in action, to God does not mean a greater degree of action; it simply supposes—and this can take us all our lives—that at the heart of his engagement the Christian places a passionate belief in the transcendence of God and is convinced that thereby the adaptations necessary will be made possible.

In the apostolate such as Christ instituted it, there must

---

[8] 1 John, 4:16.
[9] "The danger of exclusivism takes two forms. The heresy of action arises when the apostolate is confined to its external element, to a naturalising and superficial task. The apostolate may also be limited through timidity to its inner element, piety, an attitude which scarcely conforms to our Lord's words: 'It is fire that I have come to spread over the earth, and what better wish can I have than that it should be kindled?'—Luke 12:49."—Pius XII, radio message to the Barcelona International Congress of Sodalities of Our Lady.
[10] St. Basil of Cesarea, *De Spir. Sancto*, IX, 22.

therefore be as much living faith as technique, as much prayer as natural ability—or rather the first two are the condition of the second. The road to man is through God; and in that sense it is possible to say that the apostolate is beyond contemplation. It begins in it and ends in the redemption of others, which is done with God and under his influence. Far from hindering the apostle, contemplation provides him with his motive power. The apostolate therefore does not come primarily from the needs of souls but from the love of God. "The reason we have for loving our neighbor," writes St. Thomas, "is God; and what we must love in him is that he may be in God." [11] St. John of the Cross says the same: "The great love the soul has for God places it in great pain and sorrow for the small amount it does for him; and it would be largely satisfied were it allowed to die a thousand deaths for him." [12] It is this love of God impelling us to wish him to be known and loved which drew from St. Paul his cry: "*Caritas Christi urget nos:* With us, Christ's love is a compelling motive." [13]

The Saint a Living Synthesis

The two terms action and contemplation, so wrongly considered to be mutually exclusive, will not be reconciled by an abstract mixture of varying proportions. There exists a living synthesis—holiness.

The radical difference between the apostle and the propagandist is that the latter persuades and recruits whilst the former witnesses and transmits life. The abyss between the two is vast. "The Church," says Pope Pius XII, "is in greater need of witnesses than of apologists." [14]

The saint, by rigorous recollection and absolute renunciation, has stripped himself of self and allowed God to invade him; at that price and because of it he is a reminder in all circumstances of God's transcendence and of the consequences it entails. Because he has preferred the folly of Christ to ordinary

---

[11] Summa, IIa IIae, 25, 1.
[12] St. John of the Cross, Dark Night of the Soul, II, chap. 19.
[13] II Cor., 5:14.
[14] Radio speech to the Nantes Eucharistic Congress, July, 1947.

means and has left everything, he manages to regain everything.[15]

Renunciation

We remind all who, continuing the direction given to their lives by baptism, wish to dedicate themselves to action, that one condition remains indispensable to Christian asceticism. Let them remember the universal mediation of the crucified Christ. "Never seek Christ without the Cross," writes St. John of the Cross. If we follow this counsel we avoid finding a cross empty of Christ, and it is this which causes so many of our contemporaries to despair.

One primary renunciation consists, not in self annihilation, but in so living that our tendencies to evil—fatal seeds we bear within us of death—are neutralized; and for those in the world this is an asceticism as constant if less radical than a life of mortification in religion. But it is not enough for us to repair our falls by becoming more virile. The cross was not given us in order to perfect our humanism; it exacts sacrifice, a sacrifice made, by love, for God. Human failure with all its meaning must be brought into our action. Why does the latter often end in mediocrity or lack of success? Because we count solely on our own abilities instead of on supernatural means. Instead of preaching the cross, sacrifice and penance in union with our Savior, we sometimes employ methods of persuasion which succeed in obtaining us a hearing but which cause no change in the soul. Let us by all means love our brothers, and with all our strength; but let us not rest until we have prevailed on them to be converted to him. No day will end without our experiencing how true are the words of St. Paul: "It is when I am weak that I am strong. I can do all things in him who strengtheneth me." [16]

---

[15] "If spiritual men realized how much they forfeit in the abundance of the spirit and in spiritual goods through allowing themselves to indulge their appetite for useless things, they would at once find in the simple food of the spirit the attractiveness of all the things to which the will obstinately clings."—Ascent of Mount Carmel, 1, chap. 5.

[16] II Cor., 2:28.

THE MEANING OF GOD

The Remedy for Activism

The remedy for activism is contained in these last words. Beginning with a full conception of grace and of human freedom, under the name of "the heresy of action" it opens up errors which are much more ancient.

We shall have no reason to fear this error if in what we understand and do we daily have regard to the true notion of God. Because he is transcendent and his ways are past finding out we will accept failure, delay and obstacles which are seemingly impassable without surprise or discouragement. Far from crushing us, his immensity becomes the very motive of our security, our hope and our daring: "because he who is mighty has wrought for me his wonders." [17] God dwells in us and is doubly immanent in us, first as our creator then as our adopter; and for this reason we cease to count on our own weakness, the failures of which make us despair, but on Love dwelling within us who is more part of us than we are ourselves. It is his discreet and irresistible strength which works in us: "Both the will to do it and the accomplishment of that will are something which God accomplishes in you." [18]

TWO TRUTHS TO BE REMEMBERED

The saint in his own being thus succeeds in harmonizing the wealth of the two; he witnesses to the transcendence and the immanence of God, is at home in the two worlds of heaven and earth, is the man of God and a man among men. Neither an escapist nor an introvert he embodies in his own person the living image of the living God. Holiness thus becomes not merely the model but the one and only condition of a genuine and successful engagement by the Christian.

This engagement must turn on two essential realities, which form the two conditions of Christian humanism. They are the Incarnation and the Redemption.

[17] Luke, 1:49.
[18] Philip., 11:13.

THE MEANING OF GOD

Dedication: a Humanism of Incarnation

The Christian need not wait until he is a saint before engaging himself. It is enough if he is already trying, for him to have the right, the duty and the grace. Let it be clearly said once more that his title as a creature endowed with reason and placed by God as the crown of the material creation by itself gives him the right to exercise a command which must not remain merely abstract. The Gospel has not destroyed the precept which stands at the beginning of the book of Genesis: "Increase and multiply and possess the earth." [19] Man's duty is not to allow the forces of matter and of life to master him. Disorder for him would consist in his becoming their slave; it does not consist in his possessing the world; indeed from this angle possessing the world becomes for him an obligation.

Here the direction we are giving meets and repeats the appeal we made last year when we asked Christians to enter wholeheartedly into the temporal. We then grounded it on the double nature of the Church, as being unchangeable and contingent. This duty is now strengthened even further in depth and in extent by the mystery of God, as being transcendent and incarnate.

The Christian is asked not to destroy or belittle the world but to assume it and sanctify it in order to offer it as a homage to God. It is in this that real incarnation resides, in the strength of God invading humanity in order to lift it up and bring it within the sphere of the life of God; and an understanding of his transcendence illuminates this incarnation and gives to it significance and meaning. For creation itself is from him, and the element which constitutes creation is that it is a reflection and image of him. Far from despising a work as valuable as this, the Christian understands creation because he sees it with the eyes of God and loves it dearly. He makes no gesture of refusal, utters no scarcely veiled regret for the attractiveness of human values—it is more a matter of his unconcealed joy sweeping him onwards to the triumphant plenitude of the infinity of God. No humanism can be complete without faith,

[19] Gen., 1:29.

THE MEANING OF GOD

for it alone enables us to view the world from the standpoint of God; and we owe to this theological virtue, which in some way assimilates us to God's own knowledge, that we can see the created world with the eyes of its creator.[20]

We at once see on what conditions human endeavor is made possible and legitimate; it is not a question of how much, or of where, but of the spirit. Everything must be assumed in order that everything may be offered, and the movement of incarnation must be made to emerge in consecration; thereby we restore to God the universe he has entrusted to us and at once stamp this world with the sacred sign that it is meant to be ordered to him.

We find that Christ himself perfectly expressed this consecration in his prayer after the last supper: "I am not asking that thou shouldst take them out of the world, but that thou shouldst keep them clear of what is evil ... Keep them holy, then, through the truth ... Thou hast sent me into the world on thy errand, and I have sent them into the world on my errand; and I dedicate myself for their sakes, that they too may be dedicated through the truth." [21]

The feature which saves Christian humanism and differentiates it from atheistic humanism is the object towards which we try to direct it. In atheistic humanism everything is made for man and stops at man; Christian humanism, on the contrary, is theocentric: everything goes towards God, everything is for God.

Redemption: a Humanism of the Cross

The dilemma which as we saw tormented Christians, whether to be present in the world or to shut themselves up in God, thus disappears. In the terms in which it is expressed there is no solution; it has to be seen in the light of what scripture and theology teach us about God.

All however has not been said. If we were pure, if we were established in the sole love of God, our journey in the world

---

[20] "*Fides est quaedam assimilatio ad cognitionem divinam.*"—St. Thos., *In Boet. de Trim.*, qu. 3, A. 1.

[21] John, 17:15-19.

would resolve itself into nothing else than pure praise of our Creator. But ever since sin occasioned in us a tendency to seek ourselves as the end in all things, all our relations with created things can become a temptation to self-centred enjoyment, to the detriment of the rights of others and of the exclusive love to be given to God. When we forget this, we start once more a wholly material messianism, for no humanism can be built except on the recognition of sin. There can be only one legitimate humanism in the actual condition of the world, and that consists in redemption made incarnate. There can be only one humanism for the Christian, and that consists in the humanism of the Cross.

All we have said about the saint, his soul and its mortification applies here to all the dimensions of man's effort. We must remember that man is not infinitely perfectible; the dogma of original sin and the experience of actual sin are a witness to this truth. The sacrifice of Christ is at the centre of the visions of mankind. Any other solution is precarious, for it is constantly the prey to and disturbed by the disordered tendencies in man. The engagement of the Christian will only be a realistic engagement if he all the time remembers not only the "greatness" but also the "misery" of man, whom he has undertaken to serve and save.

There is only one way to correct the tendencies which constantly impell us to seek ourselves, and that is to aim straight at God by an act of filial and exclusive submission, and to prove that we choose Him before all else by accepting and choosing the road of sacrifice.

But it must not therefore be thought that in doing this the Christian renounces joy. The lives of the saints, on the contrary, show that the kingdom of God is the place of happiness in this life, and that all we may have given up for his sake will be given back to us a hundredfold. History shows how the saints who have the most died to themselves exulted at the end with love and gratitude. By firmly embracing the cross they found hope.

CONCLUSION

Having reached the end of our examination let us now turn again to the world and calmly survey it with the eyes we have been fixing on God. What we see has little relation to his peace and serenity. Confusion is everywhere, for no age has been more marked by terror than our own; and it is not easy, in these conditions, to keep the mind clear and the will calm.

Everything is in preparation, everything is in process; nothing is completed, nothing solved. Systems are built up, plan succeeds plan; so also do anguish and revolution. When order seems to reign in one place we know that in another it is attacked. The recent wars have been followed by rumors of new conflicts, and all over the world the minds of men are torn by this double madness. It is indeed stupid; but some turn this absurdity into a philosophy whilst the vast majority of men are driven by it to despair. They find no consolation after the breakdown of the ideal they had formed that progress would continue indefinitely; and they conclude that nothing can be hoped for in a world in which man is evil and fate is master.

The most tragic feature of our present distress is its silence. Millions of men are suffering, millions more expect to suffer tomorrow, yet among them there is no complaint and even surprise has ceased; they are silent. The world over, there now obtain a lassitude and a mystery which are very like the threatening calm before the fierce outbreak of the storm. No one fails to feel this anguish; we hide it, but it is there. Many of us brace ourselves in silent agony before a hideous future, and many others when told that this future is not inevitable, refused to be impressed. The evil is already vast when it grips those not yet reached by the Gospel; but if it were to conquer Christians it would constitute a scandal.

The Salvation of Man Is by God

You to whom we speak will not, we know, be among their number. Your hearts remain sensible to this universal despair, to the bloodshed and the rising tide of distress everywhere. You are aware of what your fellowmen are suffering, their sorrow possesses you, you suffer with them in the most secret places of your being. Since you feel what they endure, you can the better share their burden.

But do not fail to learn one lesson from this, that man is not saved by man alone. We do not mean that human effort is useless to cure and uplift the world; we have already said how noble is the task men on this earth perform. But the evil must be cured at its root; and since the world's sickness is not due to the absence of God, the solution necessarily lies in a return to God. The appeal we therefore make to you is thus a call to faith and a call to action.

To Action . . .

. . . because, unlike those who believe in nothing, you have no right to wait upon events when it is events which are waiting upon you. If you are absent anything may happen, because nothing stands in the way of the forces which threaten you. But if you are present you will, on the contrary, contribute by influencing the path of development, in full submission it need scarcely be said to the eternal will of God.

We say again that this is a call to action, and we ask that the return to God shall serve no one as a pretext for doing nothing or as a ground for criticizing those who devote themselves to action. Without works, faith, let it be remembered, is dead. There is no question of our doing less; we must, on the contrary, commit ourselves to the limit to action, and that everywhere. An hour when the world looks to the Christians and the Church looks to her sons is no time for the latter to betray that expectation and that confidence. Priests and layfolk are faced with a task which contains enough material to satisfy completely all their powers of love, action and self-giving.

. . . and to Faith

But before all else we must return to God in faith and never allow our trust in him to falter. We know that history is neither blind nor driven by fate—we believe in Providence. We know that evil will not triumph everlastingly over good—we believe in God's justice and goodness. We know that if we are

THE MEANING OF GOD

weak, he is strong. At a time when everything seems leagued together to drive us into fear, the example of St. Teresa of Avila encourages us to let nothing trouble us, to let nothing worry us, because God knows all, sees all and can do all—and loves us in addition.

The highest mission Christians have at this time is to pray. Do not let yourselves tire therefore in spite of the apparent silence of God, but continue to act "as though prayer were not enough" and continue to pray "as though action were useless."

In Hope

Thus instead of going from one extreme to another at the whim of propaganda and disillusioned prophets, you will never show yourselves to be "men of little faith." [22] Listen to the burning words of the prophet Isaias: "Be converted to me, and you shall be saved, all ye ends of the earth; for I am God, and there is no other," [23] and allow them to enter today into your hearts. That mighty prophetic voice reminds you, as it reminded the people of Israel, not to put your trust in Assyria or in Egypt, but in God.[24]

Confronting the rising danger and while not neglecting temporal helps, whether these come from themselves or from others, Christians will resist any attempt to reduce the present crisis to purely human alternatives. They will not look to one particular part of the universe, or rely upon another for help; they would learn too rapidly that walls of that kind crumble in their turn, and cause more ruin than they had sheltered illusion. Light and strength, they will find, stretch before them and above them, for the cure to the evils which oppress them and the secret to a new future will be found only in God. Placed by Providence on the frontiers of the world where two civilizations meet, they will be able to choose; and instead of the fickle promises of men they will prefer the pledge and reality given by God, Hope.

[22] Math., 14:31.
[23] Isaias, 45:22.
[24] Isaias, 28:33.

Prayer

"O God, who dost prepare us for the Mystery of Easter by the lessons of the Old Testament and the New, give us the grace to understand your pity for us, in order that what we now experience of your gifts to us may firmly establish our expectation of those that are still to come." [25]

[25] Holy Saturday.

GOD'S PROVIDENCE

These are times of adversity.

Are we a pawn of chance, subject to an inexorable fate, at the hands of a blind brutality of material forces? Or is there above everything here below another power, full of intelligence and love? Is there a Providence?

Let us see under what conditions we can be collaborators of God and how we can act in conformity with His plans.

Contents

Page
- 68 — I. THE ACTION OF GOD IN THE WORLD
- 72 — II. OUR DUTIES TOWARDS PROVIDENCE

God's Providence

In times of adversity each one seeks help. "Shall we find help this side of the earth?" We all are seeking, waiting, asking! Whatever the merit of the efforts expended, or whatever the value of the results obtained, can we hope for a permanent solution? Are not human things fragile, more fragile than ever in these hours of uncertainty and of inextricable difficulty?

We must, therefore, look higher. We must lift our eyes to heaven. Will help come from there? Are we a pawn of chance, subject to an inexorable fate at the hands of a blind brutality of material forces? Or is there above everything here below another power full of intelligence and love, which sees all and judges all? Is there a Providence?

The answer of certain people to this question is doubt. Many, I am happy to say, and you are among them, my brethren, know that the answer is yes. Discerning minds see in Divine Providence the supreme rule of life, and they make of this certitude a first principle for guidance.

A blessed certitude, alone capable of bringing happiness to our life! What repose can we find outside it? In the midst of so many dangers and hardships, what can our hope be except to see things in the light of God and to know ourselves guided by His hand? Blessed those who know this. Still more blessed, those who, knowing it, draw the consequences which flow from it for themselves and for the guidance of the world.

For, if there is a Providence which watches over us, our attitude must reflect it. If there is a Providence which watches over us, we have duties of faith, of gratitude, of devotion out of respect to it. If there is a Providence, which makes use of us as instruments to realize its ends, we have a duty of docility towards it. And if in its action Providence chooses certain means, or directs us in certain channels, we must try to be faithful to it without evasion.

We would, therefore dear brethren, at the beginning of Lent, help you to re-quicken in yourselves this certitude which we have from the hands of God. We would like to tell you what our attitude towards Divine Providence should be and "at what price we can help ourselves through its designs."

I. THE ACTION OF GOD IN THE WORLD

It is useless to hide the difficulties to which our faith in Divine Providence is subjected in such an age as ours. Really, we are in the midst of thick darkness. Need we enumerate the sufferings which the world bears? Who could do so? Even if we could enumerate the physical hardships of those who suffer hunger, cold, misery, and captivity, even if we could calculate the sufferings of those who fall in the field of battle, we still could not compute the principal sufferings: the moral sufferings, often hidden and therefore that much more intense since they cannot be expressed, the sufferings of hearts tired of waiting and uncertainty, broken by the sorrows of death in the family; the hardships of the country. And yet suffering still is a lesser evil than sin . . .

Suffering and sin, a sea of physical and moral illness, cover the entire world with a violence rarely experienced in the course of ages. Can we still talk about "a world order?" Can we still talk about "a supreme Wisdom," Who administers suffering and sin?

We can and we must, dear brethren. World history can bewilder us at certain times: the world exists, and it is not its own reason of existence. Events must not hide realities from us. The simplest realities, such as the flowers of the field, the birds of the air, of which the Gospel speak, testify to the existence of a Creator.

And what can we say of man's existence—his intelligence and will, at once so feeble and so great? Whence comes our indignation in the face of evil? Whence comes our thirst for justice and happiness, if we have not received them from God, our Creator? But if God creates, if He creates intellects and wills, He does so because He Himself is supreme Intelligence and supreme Love.

Furthermore, the Creator came amongst us. God became man. More than that, He became our victim and our savior. In order that we be unable to reproach Him for being indifferent to suffering and sin, He took upon Himself the suffering that

GOD'S PROVIDENCE

would deliver us from sin: Jesus Christ, Jesus Christ crucified! This is the supreme testimony to the existence of God, and to the merciful love God bears for us.

But then there is no more room for doubt: everything God has created He protects and governs by His Providence, reaching from one end to the other with power and sweetness. Everything is naked before his eyes, even things which happen through the free action of creatures.[1]

"He is our God. Our destiny is in His hands." [2] He takes care of the little and the great. He takes care of all things, for He created all things according to His Wisdom.[3] For something to escape His Providence, it would have to exist without Him.

It is not that history, which is at times so disconcerting, hides Providence, but it is Providence which alone explains history. Without the wisdom and mercy of God, history cannot explain its own conduct or its beginning and end. God did not create the world in order to abandon it to itself, as though the world could continue to exist without Him. Nothing exists unless God wishes it—and nothing happens without His ordaining it and permitting it. For He knows all, sees all, He can do all things. We know that His knowledge is Wisdom; that His will is infinite Love and that His unlimited power is embraced by His Love.

God takes care of His creatures: "See the birds of the air, they neither sow nor reap; they do not gather into barns, yet your heavenly Father feeds them." [4] "The eyes of all are turned towards Him, and He gives to each creature food in its time. He opens His hand and fills with plenitude all that lives." [5]

Would man be the only one in whom God is not interested? "You," says Bossuet, "whom He has made in His image, whom He has enlightened with His knowledge, Whom He has called to His kingdom, can you believe He has forgotten you, or that you are the only of His creatures whom the vigilant eyes of His

---

[1] Council of Vatican. (Denz. 1784).
[2] Ps., 30:15-16.
[3] Wisdom, 6:8, 11:21, 12:13.
[4] Matt., 6:26.
[5] Ps., 144:15-16.

paternal Providence do not cover?" [6] "Consider the birds of the air . . . are you not worth more than they?" [7]

We know it well: we are worth more than they. Our value is such that the Son of God has given His life for us! "We," says St. John, "have known, and have believed the charity, which God hath to us." [8]

My brethren, you also believe in the love that God bears for you. You believe in Divine Providence. May I ask you to clarify your faith?

You understand that Divine Providence works unceasingly for the world and for each of us, for to love is to wish well to the one we love. God, therefore, Who loves us, does not cease to love us well, and since He does not stop acting, He does not cease to work for our good.

God's action in the world is a secret action. God is powerful enough not to have to make a personal appearance. His invisible action manifests itself in the ordinary course of events. Hence, it does not exclude the possibility of evil. Hence, too, His action permits evil to exist and to grow, certain that the last word rests with Him and that He can draw good out of evil itself.

Have we not often seen this in history? Have we not often seen the happy result of a series of events which seemed at the time to culminate only in catastrophe? Still better do we not often see arise from catastrophe new life more splendid than what preceded it? On the ruins of the past God builds the future. He uses for this a thousand means which we do not possess and which are for this very reason the only efficacious means. Let us not ask God, therefore, to act according to our limited vision. Let us be confident in His wisdom even when it is hidden. "For my thoughts are not your thoughts. Nor your ways my ways, saith the Lord." [9] Should we be astonished that

---

[6] Bossuet, Sermon on Providence.
[7] Matt., 6:26.
[8] I John, 4:16.
[9] Is., 55:8-9.

GOD'S PROVIDENCE

His designs are inscrutable in many of their dispositions, especially the greatest of all, the redemption of the world?

After all, evil will never triumph as much as it triumphed on Good Friday, on top of Golgatha when the crucified Christ succumbed. It was the worst catastrophe of all: Israel, the chosen people, climaxed a history of infidelity. Israel, prepared for many centuries to welcome the Messias, rejected the Messias. But even this God, Who permitted it, had foreseen and announced by the mouth of the prophets; and redemption was fulfilled through this catastrophe so disconcerting in appearance. Consenting to the sacrifice of Christ, God redeemed Israel and the entire world.

If world history corresponds in the eyes of faith with the history of redemption, if the world exists only in order that God might adopt children who will partake eternally in His beatific life, must we then be astonished to have a Christ Who must suffer before entering His glory? Can we afford not to complete in ourselves His Passion in order to gain with Him new souls for Divine Life? For Divine Providence uses each of us to attain its goals and to save the world. God acts in the world by making His creatures act, each according to its nature. He did not want merely to create inanimate creatures, or living creatures without intelligence, whose unconscious actions realize without their knowing it the plan willed by Him. He created beings endowed with intelligence and will in order that they might concur freely with His designs.

If some people abuse their liberty and turn the gifts which they have received from God against Him, God never ceases to warn them or wait for them or solicit them until that moment which He has chosen for their repentence or punishment. For in the final analysis nothing can oppose His Will. Who is more powerful than God? "Who is like unto God?"

Sinners serve Providence without wanting to and without knowing it. Saints serve Providence with a love full of humble obedience, and frequently God makes known His plans to them. Let us, likewise, serve Providence in the spirit of faith, not being perturbed because we do not always see the terminus to which it leads, or even the road on which it leads us. We know that it leads us: that is enough! Peace is promised even in this world to souls of good will.

Let us conclude this first part, dear brethren, that Divine Providence is the great sustainer of the world. Providence wishes to save the world and will save it, for the world can do nothing without it and nothing against it.

This vision of faith will be for us the secret of a better course of action; a calm action, because it leans on God; a strong action, because certain of reaching its goal; an unerringly, fruitful action, because blessed by God, Who, in delaying prepares a richer harvest. Such was the life of the Saints—a St. Paul, a St. Augustine, a St. Genevieve, a St. Joan of Arc, all of whom in the most troubled times of world history worked with Divine Providence for the salvation of the world. They gave of themselves generously; they spent themselves in the completion of their task, unable to measure how far reaching their efforts were. But they called themselves "the collaborators of God"—to Whom was due the essential element of their achievements.[10]

Let us see, therefore, under what conditions we also can be collaborators of God and how we can act in conformity with His plans.

II. OUR DUTIES TOWARDS PROVIDENCE

The first duty of man, dear brethren, is to live in the truth. Nothing solid is built on illusion or deception. Let us live, therefore, in the reality of our being and of our supernatural vocation. Let us live in the truth of our relationship with God Who, having created us, does not cease to direct us by His Providence towards our final end and with us the rest of the world.

As we have said previously, however, the action of God does not suppress the action of His creatures. On the contrary, it sustains and uses it. Divine Providence does not dispense us from personal initiative. It even wishes that events which happen have the appearance of coming from us. It is right, there-

[10] I Cor., 3:6-9.

GOD'S PROVIDENCE

fore, to act according to His designs and to recognize His sovereignty. We owe to Divine Providence a concurrence of obedience and courage; but first of all, we owe it the homage of our faith and our filial devotion. Let us explain this in a few words.

If we are the collaborators of God, our first duty is to recognize His action with faith and filial confidence. To believe in Divine Providence, to have faith in God's supreme vigilance and His goodness is the homage we owe God and the foundation of all other duties. Acting on our own initiative, we must nevertheless know that we are in the hands of God, Who is our master—the *only* master of world events and our personal lives.

And if we see correctly, our faith cannot translate itself except in "filial devotedness." God is first of all a Father, a very good father to His creatures. His Providence is nothing else but paternal care, full of sweetness and wisdom. We owe Him, therefore, our confidence, and this confidence cannot be better expressed than by total surrender. To trust in one's earthly father is to leave everything to his discretion, to his prudence, and to his affection. How much more are we to do so when it is a question of God, to Whom we confide ourselves, to God of Whom we know "there is no father like unto Him."

What security, brethren, to know ourselves as being in the hands of God. What security, especially, to know that the people and responsibilities confided to us are in His hands. Treasures, which we carry in vessels of clay, are kept by God through our efforts.[11] Particularly in the difficult moments of our life when everything seems lost, it is good to turn towards heaven and respectfully and lovingly seek help from God. "I lift my eyes towards the heavens. Whence will come help? Our help is in the Lord, Who created heaven and earth." [12] "Blessed be the God and Father of our Lord Jesus Christ, the God of all comforts, who comforts us in all our difficulties." [13]

[11] II Cor., 4:7.
[12] Ps., 120:1-2.
[13] II Cor. 1:3-4.

Our faith and our filial devotion would be deceiving if it were not transformed by positive courage and obedience. It is not enough to say "Lord, Lord." [14] We must do what God requires of us. It would be better, having at first refused to do something, to relent and work, than, having said yes, to evade our responsibilities.[15]

Undeniably the present situation demands more of us than ever before. What is happening today? We must create a new order, and for this purpose we must restore our spiritual values. All values, even material ones, are deceiving when spiritual values are lacking. We must restore the spiritual values by cultivating our intellects, by disciplining our wills, by forming our consciences, by developing our moral and religious life. Can such values be restored in any way except through the fruit of our own activity? It requires all of our effort, all of our personal and collective labor. God does not replace our effort. If He consents to help us, He does so to urge us to do the work which is our responsibility, not to dispense us from it. We must help ourselves if heaven is to help us. Would any other course of action be worthy of Providence or worthy of us?

The worst of evils would be discouragement, apathy, bitterness, all of which equally hinder the work to be done. If it is already a mistake not to depend upon Divine Providence in our activity, how much greater damage would be worked if we cowardly deserted our responsibilities? This really would be an insult to God. Especially in tragic times we must beware of this.

Let us be courageous with God; but by being obedient to Him. Let us be courageous by following His impulses, by seconding His action in the world! Obedience to God, thus, is the highest homage we owe Divine Providence. This is the true testimony of our faith and filial devotion. Finally, this is the guarantee that we are not running blindly, that our efforts will be fruitful.

Obedience to God is the true way of serving the designs of Divine Providence and working for the welfare of the world.

[14] Matt., 7:21.
[15] Matt., 21:28-31.

GOD'S PROVIDENCE

For each of us, obedience to God is our only security, namely, entry into the "order willed by God."

It remains, dear brethren, to answer this very important question: If we are to obey God, how are we to recognize His Will? If our duties towards God are a matter of following His inspirations, by what sign do we recognize them? Let us try to answer with precision.

God manifests His Will, first of all, by His commandments, which outline our strict obligations, then by His inspirations and callings, which solicit our generosity, and finally by events, which reveal His Will. Commandments, inspirations, events—three kinds of signs by which Divine Providence outlines the road over which we are to be led.

It is impossible to be faithful to Divine Providence without being faithful to our daily tasks. Daily tasks are God's way of making us a partner to His plans.

The first commandment is to love Him above all things; the second, like unto the first, is to love our neighbor as ourselves. In consequence certain things are forbidden, others are positively commanded. The commandments of God and the Church make these things precise. They trace for us our duties as men and as Christians, as well as our domestic, professional and social obligations.

Everything is summed up by our duties of justice and charity. St. Paul says, "love therefore is the fulfillment of the law." [16] Are we faithful to these duties? If we do not try to be, we fail Divine Providence. Why be astonished, then, when our failures produce effects which the world must suffer?

God not only orders our life through His commandments and those of His Church, but He also does it through just, human laws. It is our duty to obey legitimate human authority. And St. Paul recommends to the Bishop that he recall this duty to his faithful. In his letter to Titus, "admonish them to be subject to princes and authorities, obeying commands, ready for every good work." [17] Having ordained human society, He

[16] Romans, 13:10.
[17] Titus, 3:1.

wants authority to exist, without which society is headless and soulless. The legitimate, constituted authority holds its mission to govern from God. From God it receives the grace to govern well, and it is God Who commands us to obey it, and to submit ourselves to its legitimate requirements is to obey God.

To be faithful to Divine Providence, let us be faithful to our duties as citizens. It is not sufficient not to oppose legitimate authority; we must recognize the powers which reside in it; we must collaborate in its effort with true loyalty; we must go along with its plans, provided they are not against the natural law and the commandments of God and the Church. Once again, when we place our confidence in the wisdom of our legitimate leaders, even beyond that which they order in strict obligation, we work within the designs of Divine Providence. The wisdom of governors, although fallible, comes from God as a providential grace.

By His commandments, by those of His Church, by the order of legitimate authority, God outlines the essential lines of the road prepared by Divine Providence. He further delineates the lines by His inspirations, which do not impose strict duties but nevertheless solicit our generosity.

For some there is the call to walk the way of the evangelical counsels. God asks them to be amidst Christian people as a light and a ferment, the living example of the pure spirit of the Gospel. All are not so called, although some callings are addressed to all, because they complete the commands of God. These are calls addressed to us by His Church.

The Catholic Church, instituted by Christ, sustained by His special guidance, is the official organ by which Christ communicates His divine intentions. Through the teaching Church Christ Himself teaches. When the Church outlines the road to travel, it is Christ, the supreme Shepherd, Who through His established ministers, leads the way for His flock.

How desirable it would be, dear brethren, if the nations were to be inspired by the thought of the Church! It is time that the world returns to wisdom, if it does not want to disintegrate in chaos. Yet we do not hesitate to say that it is on the condition of listening to the inspirations of the Church

GOD'S PROVIDENCE

that the people will survive a universal disaster and bring the world to the ways of salvation. For in listening to the voice of the Church, especially to that of the Supreme Pastor, the Sovereign Pontiff, they will follow the ways of Divine Providence and will find wisdom.

Finally, if anyone believes himself the recipient of interior light and inspiration, let him control them by aligning himself with the directives of the Church.

God solicits us interiorly and exteriorly, but He demands of us, first of all, the fulfillment of His precepts. And when an inspiration proposes even a good work, but beyond our duty, the inspiration does not necessarily come from God. It may be dictated by presumption, or even by the devil who, under the appearance of a greater good, can turn us from the true path dictated by the duties of our state. Hence, such an inspiration is known to have come from God only if it is accompanied by interior peace and true humility; and humility is, in practice, obedience to the Church.

Finally, events themselves are a means of recognizing the will of God. Providence speaks through facts. As long as events are in the future, they remain the mystery of divine good-pleasure. But once they have happened, they reveal to us God's decisions. God's commandments, completed by those of the Church and legitimate authority, call for our obedience. God's inspirations call for our docility. And God's decisions through events demand our acceptance, although acceptance does not always manifest itself in the same manner. While imposing resignation under difficult circumstances, acceptance does not dispense us from correcting evil when we are able. And if we must accept the accomplished situation which has at its origin human injustice and even our own faults, we must not allow injustice to prevail nor dispense ourselves from a sincere contrition for our faults. We must always try to avoid a greater evil and turn aside as much as possible the evil consequences or change them to a good. We correct only what we accept with patience, without revolt and without useless recriminations. We correct effectively our faults only when we recognize the evil they have caused and accept their salutary lesson.

These are the sign-posts which Divine Providence prepares for us: the only path which is certain because it is the path by which God wants us to travel. Other roads might seem wide and easy. The easier they appear at the beginning, the more likely they are to end at an impasse. To advance stubbornly in this direction is to arrive at certain disaster sooner or later. Some day or another the events will provide obstacles against which there is no resistance. You might hope to by-pass the difficulties, but the will of God cannot be by-passed. Whoever butts against the Will of God will be shattered to pieces.

On the providential road, the beginnings might be very difficult, the paths rough, and Christ has told us they would be.[18] The road at certain times might lose itself in insurmountable difficulties, but always there is a way out: God Who leads us helps us find the way out and gives us the strength to reach the end.

Let us, dear brethren, those of us who have faith in Providence, fit this faith into our lives! Let us think often of Divine Providence. Let us pray to it, and without forsaking our activity, let us lean strongly upon it. We can abandon ourselves to it with confidence, if we serve it with courage.

To those who do not have such faith, let us persuade them at least that the government of the world, of which they can see only the faint outlines, is not the effect of pure chance, but the fruit of a beneficent activity which takes care of us all and expects of us generous collaboration.

[18] Matt., 7:13-14.

THE PARISH COMMUNITY

In our century the Holy See has established the charter of the Christian laity.

A whole world must be uplifted. And the whole Christian Community must give birth to a missionary movement: missionary in spirit and missionary in action.

We appeal for an apostolate. We invite all Christians to labor in bringing the world back to Jesus Christ.

The parish is the best site for the apostolate.

The Parish Community

Each year, at the beginning of Lent, it is customary for the Pastors to address their faithful in terms of the needs of the times. We have regularly fulfilled this duty. The various subjects which we have treated always have had some connection with the apostolate of souls. And it is fitting, too, for our mission among you consists above all in assuring the spread of the Gospel. The fear-inspiring phrase of St. Paul, "For woe is unto me if I preach not the gospel," [1] applies especially to our responsibilities as Bishop. All those who, in the footsteps of the Apostles, govern the church of God, indeed are charged first of all with the salvation of souls through an enlightening of the hearts and minds of men.

Should not our faithful be kept informed of our thoughts, anxieties and hopes? We do not wish, dear Brethren, that you be ignorant of our plans. And first of all, we desire that you know the exact situation of Catholicism in the society in which you live, for we are relying on you to assist us in our apsotolic charge. You, too, have responsibilities. You, too, can render an eminent service in the propagation of the Truth. That is why the late Pope Pius XI so strongly urged the laity to the apostolate of souls.

To be sure, the faithful in all ages have cooperated with the evangelizing action of the clergy, but only in our century has the Holy See established, so to speak, the charter of the Christian laity. This magnificent work of Pius XI, which his successor, our Holy Father, Pope Pius XII, has adopted as his own, sets all Christianity in motion. It defines the form which the contemporary apostolate should normally assume. This is another reason for Pastors to keep contact with their people, in order to give them the necessary directives for a truly unified apostolic action.

The turmoil which we are now witnessing has confronted men's minds with grave problems. We are engaged in a gigantic struggle. A choice must be made between materialism and Christian or Christian-inspired spirituality. The hour approaches when it will be more difficult than ever to serve two

[1] I Cor.. 9:16.

masters. Christians, you must be perspicacious in order to discover evil under the various names by which it goes. You must be courageous, choosing resolutely in favor of the Gospel and its teachings. Now, your all-important choice undoubtedly will be made in terms of your predominant attitudes, but even more in terms of the practical orientation which you have given your life. Thought, but thought complemented and enriched by action, will in the final analysis determine your choice.

We shall indicate the broad outlines of a unified action in which all of you are called to participate. We ask that you give us all of your attention. The success of the apostolic effort, which will influence the salvation of the country, depends in a large part on the answer which you give to the urgent appeal which we address to you.

A whole world must be uplifted. What does that matter, since it must be done! Let us call to mind the famous phrase which expresses the courage of the apostles and of the first Christians who had been sent out to conquer the world; "Non admittit status fidei necessitates." "The state of faith allows no mention of impossibility." [2] That which is necessary must be accomplished. That is why we are launching our appeal! We would awaken in the minds, not only of believers but of all patriots, the salutary anxiety which will prepare the way for the resurrection. We would that all men speak often and in all social groups of the religious distress of the masses. We ask of the pastors of souls, whose mission it is to instruct and to warn, that they be the first to obey this command. We also ask that our word be taken up and repeated by all clearsighted Catholics who, because of their talents, their condition, or the integrity of their lives, enjoy a position of trust and honor in the eyes of the faithful as a whole.

As for our part, we shall strive not to fail in the duty which is incumbent upon us. "For Sion's sake I will not hold my peace." [3] So speaks the prophet Isaias. "Sion" represents the souls, all of whom grouped together make up heaven. "Sion" is

[2] Tertullian, de corona, c. 2.
[3] Is., 62:1.

THE PARISH COMMUNITY

the Church of Christ which affords refuge to the pilgrims we all are and guides us towards our goal. "Sion" is our native land, with its heritage of nobility and moral values, which are its force and the guarantee of its temporal and spiritual future. "*Propter Sion non tacebo.*" It is a misfortune to fall into despair, but it is an equally grave misfortune to base one's hopes on an illusion. Catholic opinion must be shocked out of its lethargy! Our faithful, once they have been warned, must firmly resolve to undertake everything possible to bring to Christ the souls for whom He is waiting.

THE MEANS OF REMEDY

The shock which we desire, dear Brethren, must take place first among the faithful, for the saving movement must radiate out from them. It is the duty of Christians to carry the Gospel to their brothers. It is the whole Christian community which, preserving the flame of its own spiritual life, must thereby become aware of the danger at hand, and devote its forces to saving the most abandoned souls! It must eradicate, within itself the slightest traces of religious individualism! It must give birth from within to a missionary movement, so that, by its united and persevering efforts, the wall of indifference may be broken down.

THE WHOLE CHRISTIAN COMMUNITY

Why the whole Christian community? First of all, because a work of this importance, in face of obstacles on all sides, requires action on the part of all. Also because we need to create a Christianizing environment, an environment favorable to conversions, which could not be obtained by isolated endeavors. On the other hand, these apostolic ideas, shared in common, will create a bond of charity among the faithful, will cause them all to live the Gospel more intensely. At the same time the conquering force of the Christian community will be increased ten-fold. Furthermore, if we are to reach the masses, we must necessarily penetrate all social groups, have direct contact with the individuals, study the habits and the attitudes of our brothers outside the fold, seek to discover by what approach Grace and the Gospel truths can be brought to them. Now, only the whole group of the faithful is capable of maintaining the daily contacts with the masses required by such an adaptation. And finally, if the Church is to make certain the salvation of all men, it becomes the duty of the Christian community—the daughter of the Church—to devote its efforts to the service of reChristianizing the masses.

A TRUE COMMUNITY

What, in this endeavor, is to be the task of the Christian community? First of all and without doubt, it must be a true community, i.e., not merely an artificial grouping of individuals, not a juxtaposition of isolated persons, who are joined together by a mere geographic or administrative tie, but a family, united by the bonds of a living, active charity. Although parish spirit and diocesan spirit do often exist, and even intensely among our Catholics, still we believe that in many cases there is much room for the development of both. We shall have to create among all men that fraternal union which alone can assure the victory of the Gospel: by the same token we must bring an end to rivalries between classes, groups, vested interests, and egoisms, which so often destroy all harmony and paralyze our efforts. In addition, this apostolic action carried out in common will contribute to bringing about a re-grouping of our forces, a new departure of God's chosen ones toward the promised land of a new Christianity. For we intend to ask that the Christian community be filled with a missionary zeal: missionary in spirit and missionary in action.

MISSIONARY IN SPIRIT

Now, those Catholics, who are convinced that they are God's envoys can be called "missionaries in spirit," in virtue of their Baptism and the mandate of their Confirmation. Missionaries in Spirit! Those who remember that the whole Gospel story is

THE PARISH COMMUNITY

a missionary story. The Gospel tells the story of a Divine Savior, Who came on earth to snatch men from ignorance and spiritual death; the story of a God Who spent His life on earth in calling men to penance, i.e., to conversion; the story of a God Who joined to Himself human collaborators destined to continue His work until the end of time; the story of a God Who cures bodies to save souls; the story of a God Who rejoices more over the conversion of one sinner than over the preservation of ninety-nine just men; the story of a God Who will be satisfied only when all men will have returned to the Father in the unity of life and the embrace of heavenly love.

Missionaries in spirit are those who, when observing the disbelief of the masses and reflecting on the consequences of this disbelief, are stirred within as was St. Paul when, entering Athens, he saw the city given over to idolatry.[4]

Missionaries in spirit are those who, following in the footsteps of the Master, have learned to respect and love the men who—if they only had the light—would be true sons of God. Missionaries in spirit are those who note on the first page of their Christian agenda the conversion of souls, especially the conversion of those who are nearest to them geographically.

Finally, missionaries in spirit are those who are not satisfied with desires, regrets, intentions, but who go on to acts, and who have decided to be missionaries in fact—in the practical part of their life.

The whole Christian community must go this far! Only at this price will it find itself again and live in accord with the Gospel.

THE TASK OF EACH

Cannot all members of this community be missionaries, if they so desire? Cannot each Christian take upon himself the task of converting one soul, then another, then a third? By attacking with prayers, sacrifices, kindnesses and timely interventions, cannot he count on success? Is it not possible for any baptized person to aid materially and spiritually the lay or cleri-

[4] Acts, 17:16.

cal apostles whose official mission it is to work for the conversion of the masses? We are thinking here of the groups of Catholic workers, youths and adults of both sexes, whom we should like to see active in all our parishes and who, thanks be to God, are already numerous in our diocese. During the past year did they not in a definitely deChristianized suburb reach and group together more than five hundred working girls? Elsewhere have they not reaped a harvest of scores of Baptisms and retarded first communions? But such actions and the young people who have shown so much zeal for the saving of souls do merit our encouragement, interest, affection and comprehension.

Each Catholic should desire to bring together specialized groups, or at least the various groups of "Catholic Action" (in the broad sense), within which, moreover, all the faithful should assemble themselves, whether they be members of movements or not. Without harming the necessary autonomies of specialization, such a re-grouping of the whole militant Christian community on the level of the parish and the diocese is an indispensable instrument for action. We ask, in addition, that all our groups place on their program a very precise missionary objective. We advise members of our diocese to support and, if need be, to create institutions capable of helping and guaranteeing the success of this evangelization of souls: welfare societies, centers for social and family action. Above all, to our Catholic families as well as to all our faithful we recommend the program for recruiting vocations and for giving the clergy missionary training, which affects the success of any apostolic program.

Finally, we are counting on the wisdom of the members of our diocese and on the reactions of Christians and sympathizing public opinion, in order that—without privilege or favor—France of tomorrow may be endowed with human institutions which are morally healthy and Christian inspired and which make possible the free flowering of religious values while respecting freedom of conscience. We ask that in the future the State consider the Christian faith as a treasure to be safeguarded, not as something superfluous to be eliminated. We ask that Christian ethics become the basis of social life and that, therefore, the problems of recreation, housing, religious civic planning be studied by competent men who are interested in the spiritual future of our country.

UNDER THE HOLY SPIRIT

We have not said anything, dear Brethren, concerning the apostolate, however, if we have not insisted on the fact that the Christian community must of necessity be quickened by a powerful spirit of love and a burning thirst after justice: in short, by that Gospel spirit which makes the true face of Christ shine forth. The most fruitful epochs of the life of the Church were those in which this spirit animated the masses of believers. The whole ecclesiastical community was then on the march.

Let us think of the early times of our Christian era, when young and old, slaves and masters, soldiers and merchants, Romans and Jews, Greeks and Barbarians—all faced with the same dangers of persecutions and martyrdom, rivaled with each other in zeal for the propagation of the faith. Burning with love for the Risen Christ, whose spiritual triumph they wished, they all were conquerors. Their testimony, sealed with their blood, changed the face of the world and vanquished paganism.

Let us think of the times called the "centuries of faith," when one often imagines the Church to have been at rest and enjoying a sort of tranquil hegemony over the world. On the contrary, the Church was menaced, under attack, and owed her force solely to the very bitter struggle which she was forced to wage against a multitude of enemies.

Let us think of the century of St. Louis, which was a century of crusades, i.e., another century of missions, inasmuch as Louis de Poissy, Francis of Assisi, Dominic of Guzman, Thomas Aquinas were convertors more than combattants. In spite of the roughness of their manners, the Crusaders, lords or leiges, rich or poor, priests or laity were all quickened by the same love of Christ and by the same desire to base His royalty on their common effort.

Our troubled times demand that souls once more be moved by the same breath of the Spirit. If it is to subsist, the entire Christian community must become active. A new surge must be imparted to it. Our very trials, through which God warns us to have recourse to His mercy, can make it possible for us to become the artisans of a magnificent religious renaissance.

THE WILL OF GOD

Indeed, if everything commands us to have recourse to God, in this need lies a deep reason for us to turn towards an apostolate of conquest. For, to have recourse to God is not only to pray to God, but it is also to take up the divine cause and defend it; it is also to accomplish, in so far as we are able, that which we know will be the Will of God. Now, there can be no doubt that in the present state of affairs, God's Will is that the world be freed from the materialism in which it is engulfed, and that the moral ruins, which are infinitely more dangerous than the material ruins, be repaired.

God's Will is that we consent to a powerful effort to bring back to Christ a world which is His heritage and which, be it through negligence, forgetfullness or malignity, has been stolen away from His influence. God's Will is that souls should endeavor, in order to bring relief to their suffering, to make use of the supernatural resources of their tribulations to accomplish this renaissance. God's Will is that the Church be defended by all Christians and that at no time and in no place should she be forced to suffer an eclipse which would endanger her vitality. God's Will, above all, is that Christians, following the example of Christ, stop nothing short of the total gift of themselves in the apostolate of their neighbor, since "Greater love than this no man hath, that a man lay down his life for his friends." [5]

That is why, in face of the evils which menace us and aware of the resources of generosity and devotion which are innate in our faithful, we confidently launch our appeal for the aposto-

[5] John, 15:13.

late. We ask that all Christians labor to bring the world back to Jesus Christ.

PRAYER AND BROTHERLY LOVE

In closing let us state more precisely some of the means for carrying out this apostolate.

Let prayer have the first and foremost place in it! The conversion of souls is a divine work. Those who are successful in it are those who are united with God, who maintain themselves in a divine atmosphere. By this prayer let us implore the Almighty for the cessation of the evils from which the world is suffering, the end of discord, vengeance, fratricidal struggle, the trials which are added to the tribulations of war and occupation. But above all let us pray for God to make certain the triumph of Christ and His Church. That is the only prayer worthy of a Christian.

May the members of the Christian community join action to their prayer! The apostle is a witness. When he acts under the guidance of Christ he bears witness to Christ.

To their prayer and their action may the members of the Christian community join a sincere love, a deep respect for their brothers of the working class, who are often separated from us and who must be won back to Christ. Let our faithful recognize the often unjustified suffering, the constantly increasing difficulties, the uncertainty of the morrow, which are the lot of the laboring classes! May these sentiments of brotherly love be expressed by acts, by an interest in mutual aid, by participation in any public or private initiative whose aim is to raise up the conditions of our suffering brothers. In short, may the social teachings of the Church be better known and applied in so far as possible! How can we ask that religion and Christian ethics be practiced by individuals or families who have neither home nor a minimum of material resources needed to make this practice possible.

THE PARISH

Furthermore, all should be convinced that the parish is the best site for the apostolate. This institution—the first cell in the life of the diocese—is providentially commissioned to unite souls to the Body of the Church. In addition it is provided with the required organization for penetrating the masses. From this it follows that a living, active parish community, which is coherent in its activities, and strongly united with the diocese in which the plenitude of the priesthood and apostolic ministry resides, is the incomparable instrument for the expansion of the Christian life. But for all that, the organisms which the parish has at its disposal must be regularly oriented towards the apostolate, and the parishioners must be called often to this primordial task. Further, as important as they may be, especially in areas where religious practice is abundant, the administrative and cultural tasks must never become an obstacle to the clergy and the faithful in fulfilling their missionary duty. Is this not the time to call to mind the urgent invitation of Pope Pius XI: ". . . any other endeavor, no matter how beautiful or good, must give way before the vital necessity of saving the very bases of the faith and of Christian civilization. Therefore, let the priests in the parishes reserve the greater and the best part of their strength and of their activities for the task of winning the laboring masses back to Christ and to the Church and of bringing the Christian spirit into the groups which are most foreign to it." [6]

OUTSIDE THE PARISH

Unfortunately, there are some groups which the parish cannot reach. Let us frankly admit that there is a considerable part of our population which remains impermeable to its influence. Either because of indifference, ignorance, or the individual or collective distrust of the Christian community, the Gospel message cannot be brought to these people by the ordinary methods

---

[6] Pius XI, *Divini Redemptoris*, No. 62.

THE PARISH COMMUNITY

of the apostolate. This does not mean, however, that either zeal or sanctity are lacking to those who utilize these methods. The present routine of the parish—the time which our clergy is duty-bound to devote to the service of the faithful—sometimes make it impossible for our priests to seek the most distant of those who have wandered from the flock or are not of it. Thus we insist while the parish will preserve all its rights, and must even be re-inforced in its apostolic resources, that there must be joined to it certain organizations outside the parish which will, however, work in accord with the parishes. Their aim will be to accomplish a work of missionary penetration.

We wish success to all attempts which are going to be made along these lines. We approve them. We encourage them. In so far as the pioneers of these organizations come supported by our authority, we desire that they be warmly received and be given assistance.

If our recommendations are heeded, we have reasons to believe that, since you are equipped with a doctrine, a method, well-adapted institutions and especially with a spirit, the work to which we have called you will be crowned with success.

ALL ARE CALLED

In closing, dear brethren, without forgetting that we base our hopes on the Christian community, it seems we should place ourselves on a broader ground. We turn to all who wish a resurrection of our country; even to those who do not today share our beliefs or do not actively adhere to the life of the Church, we say "Take notice, Reflect, Come to our aid!"

Take Notice. At the beginning of the encyclical, "Mystici Corporis," His Holiness, Pius XII, urges us to open the eyes of our souls: "When kingdoms and states fall, when immense resources and riches of all sorts are swallowed up in the depths of the ocean, when the cities, the villages and fertile countrysides are strewn with gigantic ruins and soiled by fratricidal struggles," [7] and when the bankruptcy of systems and ideologies is

---
[7] Pius XII, *Mystici Corporis*.

consummated on the ruins of the nations, then men, by contrast, are inclined to contemplate the Catholic Church.

They see this society of souls which remains intact throughout the storms of the ages more serene and more united than ever, preserving intact her God-given doctrine, looking down from on high on our present life while at the same time offering a priceless remedy for the evils here below. They see that she alone offers a solution capable of satisfying the desire for social justice which all of us have. They see that she alone can substitute brotherly understanding for the struggle between classes, nations, races.

Reflect! Does not this Church, so peaceful and shining in tortured times, have the word of life which will bring salvation to the world? Can you not at least consider her as an irreplaceable factor in our national renaissance? Do you not find that social and political materialism has shown its worth? That an era of spirituality must be begun at all costs? To reach that goal, you cannot leave aside the Church! That is why, in the depths of your hearts, which are so moved by suffering, separations, mourning and captivity, you feel that perhaps many standards of values must be revised. Why not, then, shake off the last bonds which hold you far from us? If you are tempted to despair, do you not know that faith can save you? If you have energy and sincerity (and we do not doubt that you have), why not cast off the errors of the past? Why not seek in the light of faith the fervor which can cause an ardor that can give life a full meaning to triumph over sarcasms and doubt?

Then, *Come to our aid!* Come, swell the ranks of those who, by word of mouth, with pen, by influence, by all the means at hand, wish to contribute to a defense and restoration of Christianity in our country!

If it be thus, then the appeal which we are launching will, by grouping in one clan believers, sympathizers, and non-believers who are seeking the light, accomplish along with the missionary task, the indispensable though difficult task of working in the service of a cause which is certainly that of our country.

THE CHRISTIAN FAMILY

In our Christian community, the family is the basic unit. We must restore our families to Christ and draw them into our missionary apostolate.

The home is the crossroad of family life, where all rejoice and grieve, where all are born and where they will die. In the home we meet and take leave of one another; we help one another in daily tasks; we learn to serve and to lead; to undertake and to persevere; there we find the model of our lives; there we are trained in wisdom and forgetfulness of self.

Contents

Page

95	I. THE FAMILY IN GOD'S PLAN
100	II. FALSE NOTIONS OF THE FAMILY
111	III. RESTORATION OF THE FAMILY

The Christian Family

The whole world is interested in the problem of the family. Citizens and rulers—and even celibates—have come forth from families or will eventually found families. Civilization itself will depend upon the family. And civilization will either progress or regress, depending on whether the primary unit of society is maintained or ruined. These things are so because the family is not an artificial thing but a reality of nature. Do away with the family and society dies. Experience confirms the theory.

In the first part of our pastoral letter, we shall determine the precise nature of the family and its place in the plan of God. In the second part, we shall indicate the principal errors concerning the family, and in the third part, the conditions for restoring full family life.

I. THE FAMILY IN GOD'S PLAN

In our attempt to bring together the teaching of the Catholic Church on family matters, we were surprised that throughout the centuries there has been very little systematic treatment of the family. We noticed the same when we looked at Revelation. The faith of Moses and the New Testament add little to the traditional concept of the family common to all civilized peoples. Long before she wrote about it doctrinally, the Church lived family life. She did not create the family, but it existed before her. When pagan converts were married—provided the union was monagamus—the Church recognized their bond. In family matters the role of the Church consisted in returning to the natural moral law, then drawing it to its highest degree of perfection. Let us not be astonished, for all of humanity is in accord: "there is no institution more natural than the family." [1] We shall see this as we consider successively *the natural law as the basis of the family; Revelation, which exalts it; and the teaching of the Church, which defends it.*

[1] Leclerq, *Principe de Droit Naturel.* T. II. La Famille, p. 6.

THE FAMILY AND NATURAL LAW

To say that the family is a natural institution is to say that it is spontaneously produced by man's biological structure and his instincts as man. Three factors clearly establish this.

The first is the differentiation of humanity into two branches, male and female, a division which was not a matter of chance but has a meaning. At the same time physical and psychical, the differentiation creates a mutual attraction between men and women which is at the basis of love. Such a union, enriching and complementary, establishes a marriage. Man and woman are joined to each other because they love each other. They are free to unite themselves. In this sense the voluntary consent which they give to each other in their choice of companions is a contract.

Once united they must submit to the conditions of the new state to which their common life has promoted them. From this point of view, marriage is an institution, a pre-established condition which one violates only by denying nature. This double character of conjugal union can be discovered in all peoples at different stages of development. Both history and ethnology confirm the value attributed to such a bond; laws surround it with a guarantee; religions, with sacred rites.

The second basis of the family is generation, which fulfills an evident intention of nature, namely, the propagation of the human race. It is to this end that the union of man and woman is ordained; it is its mysterious purpose and reason of being. From this is derived the all-important principle that their relations should be guided by the need of continuing the human race.

The birth of a child establishes the family by strengthening the union of the spouses; they are made more stable by this expression of the permanent union of their lives. It creates new relations between the parents and the new child who will extend them in life and time. Because the infant depends upon them, parents depend upon him; having brought him to light, they must feed and care for him. Among animals the union is more or less stable and exclusive, depending on the need of the

THE CHRISTIAN FAMILY

offspring; but among men, where there is a slow, difficult, and complex development of the child, the primary quality of the union of the parents is that of stability. A precarious association would endanger or hinder the life of the child. Procreation is but the first step of his birth in the world, a birth which is fully completed only at the time he enters into adult life.

Finally, in order that the child develop in body, mind, and soul, he needs a *home* where he finds brought together through the heritage of past generations the loving cooperation and double influence of both *the man* and *the woman*. It is only in their equality of rights, if not functions, that this cooperation is achieved. The moral union excludes polygamy.

Thus conjugal love, already exclusive and absolute by nature, receives from the fact of its fecundity the added notes of stability and intimacy. The normal human family is the indissoluble couple. Let us draw out the consequences of this conclusion, which does not call for an act of faith but springs from an examination of the facts alone. The advantage of this method is that on this point every sincere man can agree with the Christian conception of the family. Such an agreement is very important if there is to be a common effort at restoring the family.

THE FAMILY AND REVELATION

To remain here, dear brethren, would be to stop in route, for Christ and the Church have given to the family—without changing its nature—a nobility and a transforming grace in the Sacrament of Marriage. We express this truth when we say that the family, having been instituted by God, has been restored and made divine by Jesus Christ.

THE FAMILY, INSTITUTED BY GOD

In the first pages of Holy Scripture we see that God instituted the family. First, man was created; then, a woman is given to him as a "help like unto himself." [2] These two will be complementary beings so attracted by a mutual love that they will become one. Adam himself says so: "Wherefore a man

[2] Gen., 2:18.

shall leave father and mother, and he shall cleave to this wife: and they shall be two in one flesh." [3] Then Eve bears a son, and her motherly instinct cries with joy: "I have gotten a son through God." [4]

In these few lines, full of divine simplicity, the essential note of the human family is already presented to us. The father: reasonable, strong willed, who nevertheless has need of a woman's company. "It is not good for man to be alone." [5] The mother: intuitive, with a delicate sensibility, forgetful of self, who is the bone of his bone, flesh of his flesh.[6] The child: a fragile treasure, fruit and cause of their love, a new flame lighted from their life to burn after them.

Then, sin came, and the Bible does not let us pass over the fact that disorder entered the passions through original sin, and the family was not spared. Nor does the Bible hide from us the polygamy of the patriarchs and of many of their descendants. It shows us Moses permitting to the Hebrews "on account of the hardness of their hearts," [7] the putting-away of woman by her husband. In spite of these defections, however, the Jewish family lives on together throughout the Old Testament united and virtuous. Yet God wished for it a higher dignity.

THE FAMILY, RESTORED AND ELEVATED BY CHRIST

Hence, Our Lord restored the family to its primitive purity and elevated it to the supernatural order by founding it in a Sacrament.

Christ, first of all, abrogated divorce. St. Matthew shows Christ sending his questioners back to the first page of the Bible with finality: "What therefore God has joined together, let no man put asunder." [8] But the law seems too difficult for human weakness: "If the case of a man with his wife is so, it

[3] Gen., 2:24.
[4] Gen., 4:1.
[5] Gen., 2:18.
[6] Gen., 2:23.
[7] Matt., 19:8.
[8] Matt., 19:6.

is not expedient to marry," [9] replied the Apostles. Our Lord knows our weakness. He Himself will establish the harmony of the spouses—the essence of marriage—a Sacrament of the New Law, a source rich in the grace of unity and mutual santification, which will aid them in bringing up their children properly.

St. Paul has given us the details of the richness of the conjugal union and has extolled the model: "Let wives be subject to their husbands as to the Lord; because a husband is head of the wife, just as Christ is head of the Church. Husbands, love your wives, just as Christ also loved the Church, and delivered Himself up for her." [10]

THE FAMILY AND THE CHURCH

Thus the love of Christian spouses is not only their natural love, but the whole "love" of Christ; and the spirit of the Beatitudes penetrates and exalts it without up-rooting any of its inherent foundations.

A. THE CHURCH FATHERS AND THEOLOGIANS

In departing from inspired scripture, theologians (following the Fathers of the Church) have indicated the place of the family in the over-all plan of God. God is love. The Trinity overflows with love and wants to share it with us. From this love flows the creation of angels; from this, too, the creation and the Redemption of men flow. God wants innumerable sons, but man is not a pure spirit. By his body he is one with a world having its proper laws. One of these is that life transmits itself from the living to the living. Man is no exception. This transmission of life establishes man's dependence, but also his greatness, since on him—God having so willed it—the number of the elect will depend. God will create as many souls as man provides bodies.

Man rarely acts without a minimum of interest and rarely without love. God realizes this still better. God has infused into man a powerful and spontaneous impulse—conjugal love. He creates man and woman. They will be two in one flesh. With

[9] Matt., 19:10.
[10] Eph., 22-25.

child they will be three in one love. In this way man will be twice created in the image of God as a person and as a family. The one and the other will find in Him their ideal of perfection. The most exalted model of the family is the Holy Trinity. Man, source of life, as God the Father; woman, complement of the man, as the Word Who is the image of His substance"; [11] the child, fruit and bond of their love, like the Holy Spirit, Who proceeds from the Father and the Son. Without denying that we have here a simple analogy, let us acknowledge that the family has a privileged status and an origin which places it above all human societies. It is a provider for the City of God in heaven, and a provider for the Church, the Mystical Body of Christ, on earth.

B. THE TEACHING OF THE POPES

In the past fifty years the Popes have given the teaching on the family both doctrinal and pastoral support. We need only mention the Encyclicals and documents of Leo XIII, Pius XI, and Pius XII on marriage, the family and education. While the sovereign Pontiffs have spoken only on the occasions of attacks upon the family, they have given the doctrine depth and adaptation.

II. FALSE NOTIONS OF THE FAMILY *

Where is the family today? Does it live up to the ideal we have sketched? You know that the answer is No. In too many homes the family is completely decadent, to the point of death. The cries of alarm of the past twenty years have at least aroused public opinion.

As for the conjugal link, the first breakdown is in the practice of free love. The number of irregular unions has greatly increased, and it has brought with it more and more illegitimate and abandoned children.

How could family life itself be dragged so low? Has it thus

[11] Hebrews, 1:3.
* Editor's Note: Statistics on divorces and abandoned children in France, cited by Suhard, have been deleted, because of interest in France only.

lost all its dignity and moral conscience? In looking closer, however, one must face the evidence. The families are not themselves the blame, but the blame rests on those who, during the past fifty years, have tolerated such abuse and have sometimes concurred with it. If each individual needs a minimum of well-being in order to practice virtue, is this not more true of the family? It has, in addition, a minimum need of doctrine. Certainly no one can say that the family has found either one or the other. Rather than accuse the family, we must seek the causes of its decline.

We must find the causes, first of all, in the economic and social conditions of the family.

SALARY

One would expect, in strict justice, that the worker—the father of the family—would receive remuneration proportional to the number of his children. For a long time the head of the family has been paid the same salary as a single person. While a good number will heroically accept the inequality of a standard of living which brings misery into their lives and a lower standard for their descendants, the majority of the others retrench from such double uncertainty. Their defense is sterility, which is especially true of the one-child family. Or, the woman leaves the home to take a job.

On the question of salary, the system of family allotments has, on the contrary, brought a remedy, yet so late in coming and on such a small scale, that it is still far from assuring a parity of income.

HOUSING

Again, numerous families, especially of workers, are crowded into over-populated units, ugly and damp, cut off from air and light. Infantile epidemics and tuberculosis do their worst in such places. Worker apartments at a reasonable price, better ventilated, too often resemble barrack-buildings. The life of young couples with their in-laws, which is actually the case nowadays because of a lack of space and the high cost of furniture, deprives them of that legitimate intimacy which normally blossoms into a desire for children.

The mother of a large family, on her side, is absolutely swamped by the daily grind of feeding the family, by caring for the children, for she has none of the material things which would ease her task. When the man leaves the factory, tired and worn out from his daily work, and comes back to a dreary apartment where he is welcomed by the cry of poorly kept children and the grief of an exhausted woman, his reaction is simple: he seeks his calm and joy elsewhere. So do his sons and daughters.

Now do you see why the hovel is the great provider of saloons and the first source of family scourges.

These are all partners—they never go alone: first, alcoholism, then sports and shows which are degrading, finally, organized vice. Up to recent times these victims of vice were aided in their course by scandalous publications and by very clever propaganda threatening them with detection in their unmentionable dealings, while those who promoted it all hid behind legal statutes. With the frightening diseases born of such excesses, and especially with the perversion of souls, a whole nation is affected in its physical and spiritual health.

MATERIALISTIC CLIMATE

But it is essentially the family which finds itself undermined and dislocated. That statement might surprise some—at least those in good homes. They seem to think they are not affected by such deterioration, whose hideous visage is so often pointed out to them. Under this form they are right. But they are greatly fooled if they imagine that they and their children escape from such a materialistic atmosphere. They close the door against it, true, but they breathe it outside and even inside the home. They do not mistrust it, because evil, according to the case, knows how to be discreet, cultivated, elegant, and how to take on the semblance of respectability. To be convinced we need only state the ease with which the Christian attitude accustoms itself to divorce, if one does not guard against it. The danger is to finish by shutting one's eyes to certain moral dis-

THE CHRISTIAN FAMILY

orders which are classified as "necessary sex experience." As to the law of fertility, it is so often attacked by popular views, the novel, the theater, the movies and by vulgarization which poses as medical, that some good people come to believe, too, or they revolt against its requirements, which are called impossible of fulfillment.

Such an atmosphere would never have been created if it had not found an accomplice in legislation. The Law is said to be the reflection of morality, but on the other hand, it is also a source of it. There is a reciprocal causality, which strengthens the two individualisms. Public Law, coming from the "Declaration of the Rights of Man," sees in the nation a mere sum of individuals isolated and equal before the law, and thus it suppresses all intermediary groups between the state and the citizen. Private Law, in particular the Civil Code, consecrates this principle. It does not recognize the domestic community as such. It seeks only to assure the rights of each of its members. It limits the authority of the father; gives to the children the means to go to court against one another, or against their parents; divides the family heritage; and little by little suppresses the differences separating the "legal" family from the natural family. In short, the family is placed on the margin of the law and left to abandonment.

Juridical individualism, in its turn, has still deeper sources. It is the expression of a whole current of thought: the morality of free love.

FREE LOVE

The morality of free love finds its literary and philosophic tenets in the eighteenth century with the Encyclopedia and Rousseau. It extolls individualism, that is to say, the freedom of every human being to live as he wishes, in following the intincts of nature. This is opposed to the Christian conception of the Family, and it destroys—with equal coherence once the principles are admitted—step by step the last foundation of the Family.

Let us discuss free love, first of all. Love, as the essential form of happiness, is the supreme law; that is to say, each has the right to live with whom he wishes, when he wishes, and as he wishes. Divorce thus is no longer justified as a necessary evil —the position of its first defenders—but as a beneficial liberation. It becomes a good action which releases the couple from intolerable constraint. This does not mean, we are assured by this second stage of defense, which is that of the post-war literature—that marriage must disappear. No. It has a utility, as every contract, but on the condition of being equally revocable when the "atmosphere" of the first union no longer exists. Each one takes back his freedom—his freedom to go elsewhere.

Even this facility appears insufficient to some people, for they maintain one can desire love without desiring marriage. Marriage calls for certain conditions, financial, civil, etc. Hence, what is more beautiful than to follow nature, declare these modern "moralists"? Nature is always good. Why resist sense appeal since it is natural? It isn't free love which corrupts, they argue, but it is marriage which mixes pure love with social or interested considerations, and which condemns the spouse to perpetual slavery. In particular marriage, they say, places the woman in servitude in her submission to marital authority. "Feminism" gives her sovereign rights to dispose of her life and her being as she wishes. If the impulses of man push him towards several women, what of it? Polygamy is good, since it responds to an impulse. And what of other vices? Why are they "against nature" since they come from instinct?

But, you will object, all instinct is not good! Will not the remedy be to fight against these formidable impulses? Watch out well over yourself, they will tell you, for the sexual instinct is irresistible; to fight the passions is not to conquer them; it is to exasperate them. And in support they go on to cite, very quickly and without appeal, the axioms of "Psychoanalysis." In the name of these new principles, the "Naturalists" preach a triple crusade: war on modesty; group sex education of children; and apprenticeship in sex behavior.

In its main lines, such is the morality of free love. These conclusions alarm you, but did you not recognize them? Assuredly they are not expressed in such a logical order, but are they less dangerous? You know that they are largely responsible

THE CHRISTIAN FAMILY

for family disorder. These plagues that grip society would not be so destructive—and perhaps would never have been prevalent among you—had not these sophisms been introduced.

If you doubt this, realize that even our adversaries are alarmed as the social repercussions of the current doctrine, namely, they lead to sterility. How will "companions for a day" burden themselves with offspring? Free love—love free of children. This can be understood in two ways. If a child is inadvertently born of such a union, the parents won't object to it. They will keep it as long as it fascinates them; if it becomes troublesome, they will hand it over to the State. The essential idea is to remain free. And the surest way to do this is to remain unattached. Free love denies life. It avoids procreation by all possible means: planned parenthood—in the name of Science, they say. But there is also a cynical attack on the life of the child. A disenfranchised couple is not concerned with childbirths.

FALSE REMEDIES

Thees startling conclusions—especially the last one—have affected public opinion. There has been an effort to find solutions, but solutions purely human; in truth, false remedies, which lead us to two opposing conceptions.

NEGATIVE CONCEPTION: THE CLOSED FAMILY

Some say there is only one way for the family to avoid downfall. That is, shut itself off from the world and be sufficient to itself, to live in itself and for itself. Does not the family have this right? The family is the necessary and sufficient unit of society. Each of its members, therefore, must live for it and if need be, sacrifice his life for it. People matter little—it is the family that counts: its heritage, name, possessions. Save them and you will save the nation.

This conception presents itself both as a solution and as a thesis.

AN INEFFECTUAL REMEDY

As a solution for the decline of the family, the "closed family" idea is ineffectual and essentially negative. It flees the world and retires within itself. There is no better way to destroy oneself: "He who wishes to save his life shall lose it," we read in the Gospel. We have seen it happen to the bourgeois society of the nineteenth century and to the peasant society of the twentieth. In trying to safeguard their material interests—dowry, marriage, or heritage—they ended with an only child in the family. When it concerns large families, they maintain a defensive attitude; they give only lip service to the idea of family allotments or only awkwardly fight against an outraged morality. Such an embittered and complaining attitude discredits the role of the family in society.

As for the thesis itself, let us distinguish. That the family must be a factor of social order and stability is clear. It possesses the virtue of conservation and development which defies the wear and tear of time and men. Not in vain do we call the house a "home." In uniting children, parents and grandparents under one roof, the home peacefully unites the future and the past. The Sacrament of Christian Marriage further strengthens this stabilizing function.

HERESY OF THE SELF-CONTAINED FAMILY

But the error comes when the family stops short with its self-enclosed role, without going beyond itself. It is a social cell, true enough, but not a cell with an end in itself, selfish and idolatrous. "As great as the family is," someone has written, "it can happen that the members love it too much, serving it to the detriment of values which are greater than itself. The family, like the State, cannot be deified without harming the rights of the person." The narrow conception of the "closed family" leads to the sacrifice of the human person; it subordinates the person to a means for serving a temporal institution. We cannot admit this, since the person is the "Chosen One" in the eternal designs of God. The community—as natural and sacred as it is—is still only a means to an end. In denying this,

THE CHRISTIAN FAMILY

such total exclusiveness destroys the family itself. What becomes of a unit isolated from the whole? It slowly dies. The cell has as much need of the body as the body has need of the cells —you cannot take away from one without killing the other. Just as conjugal love cannot stop short of its purpose by forbidding the basic cell its expected growth, the family cannot mark time and vitiate the hopes of the country. Then, it is no longer a family; it is a "clan" or a "caste" which is closed to society. By its nature the family looks outward, for it is a society of people; only by playing false to its inner law does it close itself.[12]

THE STATIST CONCEPTION OF THE POPULATION PROBLEM

From such a distorted picture—which is presented as a Christian picture—one can see that Statism plays a clever hand in combatting the family. For Statism the family would serve as a brake and stabilize the social progress which other more dynamic organisms, such as unions or political parties, would have succeeded in obtaining. We must not forget this point of view, for it completely dominates Statist theory.

Yet its reasoning is cunning, for it does in fact speak of the home, family salary, domestic duties, the rights of mothers, and especially of births. One could be taken in by it, although in fact the theory is a negation of the family, pursued under the cover of propaganda.

DOCTRINAL POSITIONS: MARXIST SOCIOLOGY

A well-known Sociology says that in the beginning, there was a rudimentary society in which the family did not exist. Gradually by evolution the primitive clan developed into an actual conjugal union of father, mother and children. These, in their turn, are not eternal, but must disappear, for with the industrial civilization "all the needs which it serves will be answered by the State." [13]

The family, invented by man, could be a harmful institution.

[12] S. de Lestapis, *Valeur Politique de la Famille*. Cite Nouvelle, 20-2-41.
[13] Hesse et Gleize. *Manuel de Sociologie des E.P.S.*, p. 95.

"The first antagonism of class which appears in history," Engels says, "is that of man and woman in monogamy, and the first oppression is that of the feminine sex by the masculine." In these conditions why maintain a stable and indisoluble conjugal union?

Marxism, you see, here comes back to the doctrine of "free love," only from a different point of view.

MAN: AN ECONOMIC FACTOR

According to Marxism the essential goal of man in society is to procure for himself the maximum of goods and economic power. His first duty, therefore, will be to produce with the utmost efficiency. To do this in modern economy a regime of production controlled by the state is required. To attain its goal the regime thus must free itself of all groups which have a desire to be autonomous. In such perspectives, one sees how a domestic economy appears as a hindrance, an obstacle.

The family under its traditional form, thus, must disappear, but the association of men and women must be encouraged, for the population of the nation is at stake. Let us not be duped here. It is not the life in common which is important, but its fecundity. Just as the state has need of raw materials—wheat, iron, coal, steel—it also needs human raw material—workers for industries, soldiers for armies, etc. It needs many sane and healthy citizens. One of the first duties of the State will be to assure births. A special ministry of "Population" will watch over the increase in births.

RADICAL FEMINISM

To whom shall we look if not to mothers? How can we lead mothers to such a social duty if not by giving them special consideration? The best welcome we can give them is their emancipation from the power of husbands. And with the same stroke we impair the unity of the family. "The independence of the woman," Engels continues, "requires as a first condition their entrance into socially productive labor." In turn this condition calls for the suppression of the individual family as an economic unit of socety.

Can one be any more clear? The Right of mothers is the right to live as their husbands do. Secondly, it is the right to be unburdened of household chores which fetter their liberty as citizens and workers. Should they have children? Yes. Substantial advantage will be drawn from children. Hence, mothers are to get special considerations and all kinds of priorities. But raise their children? No. This is the concern of the State. Nurseries, kindergartens, and schools are provided.

FAMILY WITHOUT A FATHER

What becomes of the family in this vast program? It goes unmentioned, at least in its mission, for its name has never been mentioned. But in reality, a family is in question—a family without a father. Rather, the partners have changed. The State becomes father and husband. The mother is directly married to the State. As for the father in the flesh, it matters little whether he be legitimate or not. He is asked to be no more than pro-creator. We arrive, then, to a well-known phrase. "In space the family is reduced to the mother and the child; in time, to the period of nursing." This is the crowning glory of free love.

THE FAMILY WITHOUT A MOTHER

You see, then, that the State when appealing to the family in reality destroys it. Today it has need of the family; but tomorrow, if national interest would require it, it would restrict births, and this would break the last link, namely, maternity. As a matter of fact, it has already begun, since under the pretext of "unburdening the mother of her family" the State little by little substitutes itself for her. Let us not be duped by certain types of praise. It is not addressed to the family society as such—whose existence the State refuses to recognize legally. It merely wants women to bring more men into the world. The Church also invites them to do this, but for altogether different goals: the State wants more "man power." The Church wants "children of God."

THE CHURCH AND POPULATION

This essential distinction sets apart the position of the Church on the family from the position of the State. To the latter the Church concedes a role: the family normally cannot do without society. "The family," says Pius XI, "is an *imperfect society*, because it does not have in itself all the means necessary to reach its proper perfection." Here is the condemnation of the closed family, while, the Pope continues, "the civil society is a *perfect society*, since it has in itself all the means necessary to its proper end, which is the temporal well-being. It has, therefore, under this aspect, pre-eminence over the family." [14]

THE FAMILY: AN IMPERFECT SOCIETY

An imperfect society signifies, on a juridical level, that the State has the right and the duty to recognize and guarantee the conjugal bond; to protect the offspring; to complete the education of children in the measure in which the parents give it the mandate, and according to the choice they express. Thus, the aid of civil society is indispensable to the full flowering of the human person. It offsets the disadvantages that a life would have if it were restricted to a family circle; it responds to the need of the young to face the world.

Someone has said, "It is a false and dangerous belief to expect the family to be sufficient in everything for its members, and to refuse to the children the right to look outside the family for inspiration, friendship and support. The family is everything for the young children—nothing truly replaces it. But in the eyes of adolescents it nearly always becomes too small a world, whose doors they are impatient to open."

But to conclude from this, as does Statism, that the family is not useful or a nuisance is to play with words. The family is not an artificial invention of society; the historical arguments which support this contention more and more are disputed. Ethnology discovers the domestic society under its actual form among the most primitive peoples. "Historically, the state ap-

[14] Encyclical, "Christian Education of Youth."

pears after the family. It is not the State but the family which first of all came into existence. A nation is but a community of families. The family is the source of society." [15]

The family, one and indissoluble, far from being the impoverished residue of society, is indeed a living source of energy, a force which proceeds from its interior love to diffuse itself. The family is love perpetuating itself in an institution, which the whole history of the world proves.

Let us cite these few clear affirmations of the recent Popes: "The source and origin of the family and of all human society is found in marriage. If one considers its object, God has evidently put in it the most profound sources of the public good and welfare." [16] Pius XI says that "the state is what families make it to be." [17] To inject secularism into this "mother cell" is to infect the whole social body, since his Holiness, Pius XII, states: "the family is not only the cradle of children, but also of the nation." [18] We are far from the "closed family."

Because of your faith, the issue is clear for you, my brothers. It is also clear to every right mind. There is no reason for hesitation. Before such a great reality and before such grave heresies against which we warn you, in face of a diminution of family life, there is one outstanding duty: we must all contribute to the restoration of the family.

III. RESTORATION OF THE FAMILY

The task before us is immense. Yet it would be entirely false and unjust to believe that nothing has been done about it. Courageous attempts have born fruit. After so much evil these efforts are our hope and our joy. We must recognize that due to them we have undoubtedly changed some things for the better.

When we say that the Christian family has taken on a new vitality, we do not imply that such progress has reached all

---

[15] Declaration of Cardinals and Archbishops, Nov., 1945.
[16] Encyclical Arcanum.
[17] Encyclical, "Casti Connubii."
[18] Allocution, 1942.

Catholic families, nor even the majority. Nor do we mean to insinuate that something new has been added to the Sacrament of Marriage. We wish only to rejoice in realizing that an increasing number of families are imbued with a family spirituality and are living it intensely. Our gratitude goes out to all the Family Movements which by their object, methods, publications and meetings have sparked this renewal. Our thanks to all the families, young and old, who have taken this spirituality to heart and applied it to their lives. We are happy to cite them as examples.

A DEEP CONJUGAL SPIRITUALITY

Without speaking of the nuptial ceremony, in which the worldly extravagances of late have given way more and more to prayerful Masses with Holy Communion, many spouses today look for and find in their union the secret of true Christian perfection. They realize the two ends of marriage which the Code of Canon Law and moral theology teach them: their homes are united and fruitful. Following St. Paul they especially insist on the sublimity of their union. They give legitimate value to the physical aspect, and that without Jansenism. But they also know the beauty of continence, and generously impose restraint on themselves. Body and soul play their proper role. Union for these spouses is the instrument of transforming graces. Marriage is a vocation and a state of sanctity. Recent inquiries show to what heights a love thus understood can elevate two souls.

FAMILY SPIRITUALITY IN COMMON

These inquiries also show what a family centered in Christ can accomplish. Let us cite solely the happy effects in the religious life of the family: evening prayer in common, reading of the Bible, preparation of and assistance at Sunday Mass, etc. Many parents seek to give the Christian meaning of family living to their children during times spent together in a family way, such as at meals and at evening, at work and leisure, at special times such as births, sickness, funerals. They also seek to create a Christian atmosphere by the appropriate decoration and arrangement of their home, by the participation of everyone in family prayer, and in the daily chores done in the service of the family and by giving a new emphasis to the sacraments, particularly those having a family significance: Baptism, the Eucharist, Marriage, Extreme Unction.

CATHOLIC ACTION AND FAMILY SPIRITUALITY

Such families merit the name of homes. They radiate. In reviving true family living they spread their good influence to the nation as a whole. Family restoration is both an effect and a cause: an effect, because it owes its origin to the Catholic Action movements which have taught their militants to put "the whole Gospel into their whole lives." In return it becomes a cause in giving to this same Catholic Action its modern form—Family Action. In its beginnings Catholic Action counted as its members only young apostles who were single. Today these are the fathers and mothers of families. Catholic Action is no longer in its beginnings; it leaves its adolescence and enters adulthood. It has a family footing at marriage age.

In the beginning the specialized Catholic Action movements were defined as the action of worker on worker, student on student, but now, with much logic, the motif is "conquest of family by family." Do not believe, however, that Catholic Action disavows for this reason its first method of an apostolate for the young. No. It simply follows the movement of life and grows with life. It becomes family action in the home. It evolves in order to remain true to itself—always adapted to new times and new needs.

The cooperation of families in the apostolate of the hierarchy is a fact without precedent. It constitutes a veritable revolution—the progressive victory of the community spirit over individualism, a step forward towards the realization of the Mystical Body of Christ.

It assumes two forms. On the plane of spirituality one sees more and more Catholic homes reuniting periodically in groups for a triple purpose: prayer in common, mutual spiritual and material aid, and the study of family problems. This formation is also sought in days of recollection, at family retreats, through specialized literature.

On the plane of action, they aid in instilling Christian Family ideals in their daily lives and works. They want to Christianize the whole life of the home. To do this they bring the aid of the large Christian Family Movement to bear on the problem; they bring in addition the testimony of their own family, and in each locale they assume the responsibility for bringing families together in a common ideal of mutual aid and restoration.

Here again we are in the presence of a new fact: the restoration of the whole country by the constructive work of united families and then by the testimony of individual families.

THE DUTY OF FAMILIES

Families, first of all, must recognize themselves and become aware of the force which they represent in the nation. Now, it is precisely this which the majority of families do not understand. They have a disdain for family associations, which they view simply as an effort to increase birth rates and which they suspect of political intentions. For such reasons family associations have so few members. Is there need to tell you that when we ask you to participate in such groups, we do not leave the family level? Families that group together have but one aim: to form a Family Corps which could speak in their name and promote legislative and social action which will save the nation while restoring its primary unit, the family. With grass-roots strength, this organization will render a great service to the nation in making lighter its tasks and also a great service to the people in restraining state socialism.

SOLIDARITY AMONG FAMILIES

Solidarity among families requires faith. Families must forget their timidity and their inertia and inspire themselves with a militant family spirituality. We address very especally those of you who are heads of families, whatever be your social status, professions, or size of family. We ask you to enter immediately one of the already existing family movements. We do not hesi-

THE CHRISTIAN FAMILY

tate to urge you to do this as a grave duty in conscience. We insist on this all the more since the Family Corps is at present the object of sharp competition. You must not let it be turned from its mission. Your only means to do this will be to make your presence felt and to act as militants in the cause of the family. This calls for action rather than words. You will generously undertake the services of your association which best respond to your talents.

In giving you the watchword we again take up the instructions that His Holiness Pope Pius XII addressed to French families on June 17, 1945, and to the Catholic women of Rome, October 21, of the same year.

"Fathers of Christian families, it is your right and your duty to act and to speak in the name of your families." "Catholic women, will you leave . . . to those who become accomplices in the ruin of the home . . . the monopoly of the social organization in which the family is the principal element? The destiny of the family, the destiny of the human community, are at stake; they are in your hands. Each woman without exception thus has the duty to act (under the forms most suitable to the condition of each), to restrain the influences menacing the home, and to organize and effect its restoration. Your hour has come, civic life has need of you."

THE DUTY OF THE STATE

The road has been mapped. The duty of families is to prepare the State for its duty of family restoration, instead of passively awaiting a miracle. Thus facilitated, the task of the State is immense. Its object is not merely to repair flaws in family life—this would be a short-sighted policy, unworthy of the times in which we live. The State must found the whole national reconstruction on the family by developing a family platform.

A CIVILIZATION BASED ON THE FAMILY

This is a large perspective, since the whole new civilization must be conceived, if it is to carry on, in terms of the function of the family, taken as the basic unit.

This means, first of all, the legal recognition by the Constitution of the Family as a social reality and a juridical institution. This quite naturally brings up its representation in the councils of the State. In legislation, there must be a forward step towards the suppression of the divorce law, the energetic abolition of abortion, a fight against alcoholism, immorality, organized vice, etc.

These measures of physical and moral purification will have a better chance of success in the framework of civic pride, conscious of the lessons of the past, in full-bodied, constructive civic planning. Small or medium sized villages are to be preferred to gigantic cities. Lodging is at once spacious and more friendly; work is more wholesome and less nerve-wracking; and life has more of a family atmosphere.

TRUE FEMINISM IN THE FAMILY

The salary of the father ought to be sufficient—with a perfected system of family allocations—to raise the level of existence of a large family to that of single workers and to permit the mother to remain in the home without dire financial difficulties to her family. The problem of Feminism ought to be orientated to this goal. No one asks that woman remain walled in her home, but that the home be given a culture and activities compatible with her family duties and centered on her inherent qualities as wife and mother. In the present actual conditions of a large family, such a balance is impossible.

Not that a lack of maturity kills it, but rather poverty, or a lack of assistance throughout her long sixteen hour day. The State also must consider as one of its most urgent duties the problem of Family Aid. In helping organize it, the State should be on guard not to replace the mothers with a substitute, but provide mothers with social workers who have a philosophy favorable to family life.

Let us also mention that the State must respect the rights of parents in education and make the school a natural complement of the family.

On the role of the civil authority in the restoration of the family we have indicated several suggestions, without a formal

THE CHRISTIAN FAMILY

listing and without prejudice to a particular technique. These suffice for us to conclude that a family policy, far from being a secondary duty of the State, should be a Welfare Policy looking to the future. Let those who have assumed the heavy responsibilities of government be persuaded of it and busy themselves in effecting it.

THE DUTY OF CATHOLICS

Doing this, we have not resolved the problem. The essential factor remains in the family itself. For if certain economic and social conditions are necessary for the development of the family, they are not the cause of it. You know quite well that certain homes equipped with all home appliances remain engulfed in voluntary stagnation. Why? Because they have no principles. We always come back to the absolute need for a spirituality.

Thus, we count on you, our faithful Christians, to bring about this great "Return to the Family."

To spouses and Christian parents, we ask that they restore the principle of authority in their homes—conjugal and paternal: the husband having the "primacy of government" and the wife having the "primacy of love." Let them not give way, either, to a "fear of life," as plausible as that might appear. Providence is there.

To future spouses, we ask that they prepare themselves, separately at first, then as fiancees, for the work which awaits them. We heartily encourage them to take part in conferences and retreats of formation which have been especially prepared for them. As for Baptism, Holy Eucharist, and Holy Orders, so too does the Sacrament of Marriage require preparation. In this area much yet needs to be done. Parents and educators must see to it.

The movements of Catholic Action find a role to play, too. They have already played it, and played it well. We recommend that they be careful not to separate the movement of young people from the movements of married adults.

Finally, our priests must quicken their zeal and strengthen themselves in doctrine in order to bring about the restoration of the family. It is desirable that in their seminary training they receive the element of family pastoral theology and that they use and deepen these principles in the future. They can become competent chaplains for family groups, in which we see the signs of restoration.

The whole Church—families, Catholic Action, and the clergy —must bring about a great renewal of family life. This is the mission of the Church, and the Christian family lives up to this purpose.

FULL FAMILY LIFE

We all know that Christian families form a front. They are distinguished by a "family attitude" from the eldest to the baby in the crib. Their special family seal is the mark of great love; it is the sign of long patience, the patience of successive generations; the sign of the never-tiring efforts of the two spouses. Their sons and daughters surround the spouses at the dinner table "as young olive plants." [19] No one is rich, since everything is shared; no one is poor, since all is held in common. Love, especially, gives itself abundantly. There is the peaceful love of the grandparents in the evening of their lives; a faithful and deep love of the spouses for each other; a mutual exchange of maternal and filial love. The home is the crossroad of family life, where all rejoice and grieve, where they are born and where they die. In the home we meet and take leave of one another; we help one another in daily tasks; we learn to serve and to lead; to undertake and to preserve; there we find the model of our lives; there we are trained in wisdom and forgetfulness of self. Our home is the school of duty and human virtues.

THE PERFECT FAMILY IS THE CHRISTIAN FAMILY

Who will deny that these virtues are also Christian? They are Christian in their culmination, for supernatural life cannot do without them. They are the foundation of the supernatural life. But they are Christian especially in their origin, for they

[19] Ps., 117:37.

THE CHRISTIAN FAMILY

are born only of the cross of Christ. The family is founded on sacrifice.

Only a Christian conscience, attached to its divine origin, is capable of such renouncements. It alone can inspire the couple to fidelity of body and soul during their whole life, in spite of the concupiscence born of original sin. Generous and mortified souls alone can accept the risks and burdens of child-bearing. They alone are capable of raising a large family in honor and making men of them. The happiness which radiates from these families is not of this world. Its source is elsewhere, in a joy which comes from God.

CONCLUSION

The happiness of a family is a joy which comes from Christ. It is He Who blesses them. It is He Who is the soul and life of the family. Grant that He animates them, that He be the source and term of them. That is our wish and prayer. Then, "Christian Families," grouped "by the thousands" to "ardently promote the reign of Jesus Christ" can be confident and say once again with the Holy Father: "Who will match the power of such an army, under such a leader?" [20]

PRAYER ON FEAST OF THE HOLY FAMILY

"O Lord Jesus Christ, Who, in the days of Thy subjection to Mary and Joseph, didst consecrate home life by ineffable acts of virtue; by the intercession of Thy Holy Mother and Thy Foster Father, make us so to profit by the example they with Thee have set for us, that we may be counted members of Thy household for evermore. Amen."

[20] Pius XII. Discourse to French Families, 6-7-45.

FIDES **DOME** BOOKS

D-1 GROWTH OR DECLINE, Emmanuel Cardinal Suhard. The State of the Church in the Modern World. (95¢)

D-2 MORE THAN MANY SPARROWS, Leo J. Trese. A Practical Guide to Christian Living. (95¢)

D-3 WHAT CATHOLIC GIRLS SHOULD KNOW ABOUT MARRIAGE, Francis X. Dietz. A Review of Catholic Teaching on Marriage. (95¢)

D-4 ACCENT ON PURITY, Joseph E. Haley, C.S.C. An Illustrated Guide to Sex Education. (95¢)

D-5 WISDOM SHALL ENTER, Leo J. Trese. A Course in Catholic Apologetics. (95¢) With Discussion Questions.

D-6 MENTAL HEALTH IN CHILDHOOD, Charles L. C. Burns. A Nontechnical Discussion of Problems with Maladjusted Children. (95¢)

D-7 PRIESTS AMONG MEN, Emmanuel Cardinal Suhard. On the Priestly Mission in the Modern Social Order. (95¢)

D-8 PURITY, MODESTY, MARRIAGE, Joseph Buckley, S.M. A Christian Design for Sex. (95¢)

D-9 SIGNS OF LIFE, Francis Louvel, O.P. and Louis J. Putz, C.S.C. The Seven Sacraments. (95¢) With Discussion Questions.

D-10 CHRISTIANS AROUND THE ALTAR, The Community of St. Severin. The Mass as the Sacrament of Unity. (95¢)

D-11 MODERN MORAL PROBLEMS, Msgr. J. D. Conway. Catholic Viewpoint on Controversial Questions. (95¢) With Discussion Questions.

D-12 MANY ARE ONE, Leo J. Trese. Christ in Daily Life. (95¢) With Discussion Questions.

D-13 WHAT IS YOUR VOCATION? Brother Andre, S.C. and Joseph H. Maguire. A Guide to the Priesthood, Religious Life, Marriage, and the Single Life. (95¢) With Discussion Questions.

D-14 THE TRIUMPH OF CHRIST, A. M. Henry, O.P. The Word Made Flesh. (95¢)

D-15 THE MEANING OF MARRIAGE, Eugene S. Geissler. Sex, Love, and Life—I. (95¢) With Discussion Questions.

D-16 THE MEANING OF PARENTHOOD, Eugene S. Geissler. Sex, Love, and Life—II. (95¢) With Discussion Questions.

D-17 WHAT THEY ASK ABOUT SIN, Msgr. J. D. Conway. Moral Theology, the Commandments, and the Virtues. (95¢)

D-18 THE ADOLESCENT BOY, W. Connell, S.J. & J. McGannon, S.J. Trying To Get His Point of View. (95¢)

D-19 CONVERSATION WITH CHRIST, Peter-Thomas Rohrbach, O.C.D. An Introduction to Mental Prayer. (95¢)

FIDES **DOME** BOOKS

D-20 LEND ME YOUR HANDS, Bernard F. Meyer, M.M. A Popular Guide for Parish Catholic Action. ($1.25) With Discussion Questions.

D-21 THE CREED—SUMMARY OF THE FAITH, Leo J. Trese. Volume I of the Faith and Christian Living Religion Program. ($1.25) With Discussion Questions.

D-22 SALVATION HISTORY AND THE COMMANDMENTS, Leo J. Trese and John J. Castelot, S.S. Volume II of the Faith and Christian Living Religion Program. ($1.25) With Discussion Questions.

D-23 THE SACRAMENTS AND PRAYER, Leo J. Trese. Volume III of the Faith and Christian Living Religion Program. ($1.25) With Discussion Questions.

D-24 GUIDE TO CHRISTIAN LIVING, Leo J. Trese. Volume IV of the Faith and Christian Living Religion Program. ($1.25) With Discussion Questions.

D-25 THE PSALMS, Fides Translation. Introduction by Mary Perkins Ryan. A Clear, Modern Translation. ($1.25)

D-26 MARRIAGE IS HOLY, H. Caffarel. Essays on the Spiritual Aspects of Marriage. ($1.25) With Discussion Questions.

D-27 MORNING PRAISE AND EVENSONG, William Storey. A Popularization of the Two Major Hours of the Office. ($1.25)

D-28 A MAN APPROVED, Leo J. Trese. The Priest and His Vocation. (95¢)

D-29 ST. PAUL—APOSTLE OF NATIONS, Henri Daniel-Rops. A Fast-moving Biography of St. Paul. (95¢)

D-30 WOMAN IN THE MODERN WORLD, Eva Firkel. An Appeal to Feminine Human Nature. (95¢)

D-31 YOU ARE NOT YOUR OWN, Dennis J. Geaney, O.S.A. The Mystical Body in Action. (95¢)

D-32 THE MEANING OF GOD, Emmanuel Cardinal Suhard. The Meaning of God, God's Providence, The Christian Family and the Parish Community. (95¢)

D-33 FOR MEN OF ACTION, Yves De Montcheuil. Spiritual Guidance for the Layman. (95¢)

D-34 SEEDS OF THE DESERT, Rene Voillaume. Living Like Jesus of Nazareth. (95¢)

D-35 GOD SPEAKS TO MEN, Thomas Barrosse, C.S.C. Understanding the Bible. (95¢)

D-36 THE MODERN APOSTLE, Louis J. Putz, C.S.C. About the Vocation of the Layman in the Church. (95¢)